Psychology and behavioral medicin.

Psychology and behavioral medicine

S. J. Rachman (Stanley Jack)

Clare Philips

Institute of Psychiatry
University of London

Cambridge University Press

Cambridge
London   New York   New Rochelle
Melbourne   Sydney

Published by the Press Syndicate of the University of Cambridge
32 East 57th Street, New York, New York 10022, USA

Hard-cover edition published in Great Britain by Maurice Temple Smith, Ltd.,
London, 1975, under the title *Psychology and Medicine,* and distributed
in the United States by Transatlantic Arts, Inc.
British Commonwealth paperback edition published by
Penguin Books, Ltd., London, 1978.
Revised hard-cover and paperback editions published in the
United States and Canada by the Cambridge University Press, 1980,
under the title *Psychology and Behavioral Medicine.*

Printed in the United States of America
Printed and bound by Lithocrafters Inc., Chelsea, Michigan

Library of Congress Cataloging in Publication Data
Rachman, Stanley.
Psychology and behavioral medicine.
First published in 1975 under title: Psychology and medicine.
Bibliography: p.
Includes index.
1. Medicine and psychology.   I. Philips, Clare, joint author.   II. Title.
R726.5.R32   1980   616'.001'9   79-8589
ISBN 0 521 23178 7 hard covers
ISBN 0 521 29850 4 paperback

Contents

Foreword

Behavioral medicine, the application of the behavioral sciences to the broad range of medical problems beyond those psychiatric disorders with which clinical psychology has been traditionally concerned, represents a significant development in the improvement of health care. The term "behavioral medicine" was unknown only a few years ago, yet today clinics, laboratories, and programs devoted to behavioral medicine are springing up throughout the country. The upsurge of interest has been dramatic. In April 1978, the Academy of Behavioral Medicine Research was founded under the auspices of the National Academy of Sciences, and later that year the more broadly-based Society for Behavioral Medicine was formed. Books and articles are proliferating, and a new journal devoted exclusively to behavioral medicine has already begun publication. There seems to be little doubt that behavioral medicine is an important coming together of behavioral and biomedical sciences in an endeavor that has potentially far-reaching consequences.

Of all the books in this new field, none provides a better introduction than the present volume by Rachman and Philips. The authors bring impressive credentials to their task. Rachman is already established as one of the world's leading authorities on the application of psychological principles to behavioral disorders, and both he and Philips have made significant contributions to the growth of behavioral medicine. They tackle with unusual success the difficult task of combining theoretical sophistication with comprehensive coverage of the major areas of practical application of psychology to medical disorders. In addition to an informed discussion of the now standard areas of application in behavioral medicine, namely, the treatment of problems such as pain, headaches, sleep disorders, and stress, the authors also provide valuable new information on the seminal but still curiously neglected subject of doctor–patient communication. Related to this topic is the vitally important issue of compliance, or what is now known more euphemistically as adherence to therapeutic instructions. Our success in encouraging patients to take necessary (and effective) medication to control disorders such as diabetes or hypertension, for example, will significantly affect health care practices. One of the most promising lines of inquiry in behavioral medicine is the focus on improving patients' adherence to therapeutic instructions.

New fields of research and practice inevitably are attended by much hoopla and hard-sell on the part of uncritical "believers." As Neil Miller,[1] a pioneer of biofeedback and now a major figure in the development of behavioral medicine, has cautioned, "The increasing interest in behavioral medicine opens up significant new opportunities for research and applications, but there is a danger that over-optimistic claims or widespread applications without an adequate scientific base and sufficient evaluation by pilot testing can lead to failure and disillusionment. Such disillusionment could block the promising developments in this area for another generation" (1979). Happily, Rachman and Philips are refreshingly circumspect in their evaluation of the current status of behavioral medicine. Seasoned professionals, they are careful to distinguish between fact and fancy, and offer a balanced analysis of what advances have been made and what areas of ignorance still exist. Importantly, they indicate how the theory and methodology of psychology can be brought to bear in those areas where we cannot as yet provide specific guidance to the practitioner in order to find the answers. There is something here for the researcher as well as those with more applied interests or simple curiosity. Last, but hardly least, the authors are to be congratulated on the lucid and readable style in which they cover so diverse a range of technical and scientific subjects without sacrificing scholarship. This is a book that students and professionals – psychologists and physicians alike – will enjoy reading.

G. Terence Wilson

Rutgers University
October 1979

Acknowledgment

We wish to thank Mr. W. Glazier and Professor Neal Miller for kindly granting permission to quote from their work, and their publishers (The American Association for the Advancement of Science and The Scientific American, Inc.) for their agreement.

1 Introduction

Behavioral medicine is a new and rapidly growing branch of medicine. Like other areas of medicine, it has its theoretical and practical sides. The psychological and social determinants – and the defining characteristics of – "illness" and health, and of therapeutic processes, are the basic theoretical problems. On the practical side, behavioral medicine encompasses the study of the psychological and social factors that influence health-care decisions, preparation for medical procedures, communication between patients and doctors, acceptance or rejection of pharmacological and behavioral prescriptions and advice, the process of recovery, the use of preventive measures, and so on. The practical problems are of immediate interest, but theoretical developments promise to effect profound and enriching changes in the theory of medicine as a whole. This book provides an overview of both.

The great social reformers achieved a clear understanding of the connection between socioeconomic conditions and health, and successfully argued that improvements in living conditions would alleviate or prevent many illnesses. All of us are beneficiaries of their perspicacity and drive. Epidemics are rare, the killer diseases of past centuries have been tamed, and infections are no longer a major cause of death.

However, in one important respect the predictions and hopeful expectations of the social reformers were seriously deficient. Improvements in living conditions and the associated conquest of infectious diseases did not lead to a declining need for health services. The great paradox of modern medicine is that improved health has been accompanied by *increasing demand* for health services. This totally unpredicted paradox is to a considerable extent rooted in psychology.

Improvements in living conditions have been accompanied by growing psychological needs (and expectations) for the relief from, or even the total avoidance of, discomfort. Our psychological tolerance for physical discomfort, including minor illnesses or disadvantages, has declined steeply. Hence, desire for care and comfort, especially from professionally trained personnel, has grown rapidly. The range of complaints and discomforts that we can legitimately take to the doctor's consulting room grows wider – a development that carries the seeds of considerable difficulty and dissatisfaction.

The psychological component in illness and discomfort enters into the very definition of what constitutes an illness. It plays a major role in determining what action is taken by the affected person or by his relatives or friends. It has a major influence on how the doctor or other health workers respond to the person and his problem. This psychological component determines if the patient acts on the advice or instruction provided–and recent evidence shows that an astonishingly large amount of professional advice is ignored. Contrary to appearances, effective medical action does not terminate with the issue of a prescription.

Recognition of the need to adopt a more comprehensive view of the theory and practice of medicine than that embodied in traditional medicine is evident in the timely growth of *behavioral medicine.* Medical care can be improved for everyone if the ideas and methods of modern psychology are successfully incorporated into the practice of medicine. At present most people pay lipservice to the idea that psychological factors are important in health and illness, but little action is taken. One of the aims of this book is to present the arguments for action and a variety of proposals as to the form it might take.

Before we attempt to show why and how we believe that psychology could enrich medicine, we must try to deal with a confusion about what the word actually means. Many people interpret psychology in a medical context as being synonymous with psychiatry, and therefore as being concerned with mental illness. The phrase, "it is psychological" or, more commonly, "it is only psychological," is used to dismiss symptoms for which doctors can find no physical cause. Patients interpret such statements as meaning that they are thought to be inventing their discomfort or experiencing it only because they are "neurotic." Relatives, and even doctors themselves, often feel that this pat phrase relieves them of part of their responsibility for the patient's care and comfort. If it is "only psychological," then it has no "real" (i.e., physical) cause, and they cannot be expected to help the patient obtain relief. The extreme of this attitude is illustrated in the story of the sergeant who reported to his commanding officer: "No additions to the sick roll, sir, but regret to report that another three malingerers passed away during the night."

Psychology describes the behavioral, subjective, and psychophysiological components of human experience both in health and in illness. When something goes wrong with an individual's mental functioning, the illness is the province of the psychiatrist. When something goes wrong with an individual's bodily functions, the illness is the province of the doctor. Either type of dis-ease will affect the patient subjectively, so in either case the psychologist should have a contribution to make to his or her well-being.

The fact that this claim is not taken sufficiently seriously is partly the fault of psychologists themselves. Since the beginnings of their profession they have confined most of their clinical work to psychiatric disorders, neglecting the rest of the spectrum of health problems. We are confident that a broader application of psychological ideas and methods will benefit them as well as patients, their relatives, and doctors. If the infusion of psychology is carried out satisfactorily, it may well lead to improvements in some current medical theories. It may also contribute to the restoration of a balanced perspective on medical practice – a balance that has been distorted during the recent period of rapid technical advances.

Developing a psychological view of medicine means reexamining our very definitions of illness and health. As we hope to show, many doctors and most patients think about many health problems in a way that is out of date and therefore unrealistic. Some of these misconceptions shore up inefficient and outmoded practices. They obstruct the introduction of the major changes that will be needed if we are to provide effective and humane care and comfort for people in need.

We believe that the next few years will, and must, bring about a gradual change in the style of medical practice. Doctors will discard their paternalistic attitudes and learn to communicate, frankly and freely, with patients whom they see as equals. Patients will have to reciprocate by taking a greater share of responsibility for their own care, using their doctors as advisers rather than as instructors. Psychologists will also need to change their professional attitudes and practices. Far more of their research effort will have to be devoted directly to human problems, even at the expense of their long-standing devotion to the worthy but pampered laboratory rat. For economic, social and ethical reasons, doctors, psychologists, and all those in the professions related to medicine will be required to account publicly for their actions and their policies. It will no longer be sufficient to account to professional colleagues in private. They will have to account also to the patients they are trained to serve and to the community that pays them.

The nature of health care and the demands upon it, have altered radically in the last few decades. In its early stages modern medicine had to contend with episodic, usually infectious, illnesses. These are virtually defeated. Contemporary medicine has to deal instead with chronic disorders and disabilities, especially among the elderly. The role of psychological factors is especially important in chronic disorders; the need for a psychological approach to medical care has grown with this shift, and it is in this area that psychologists can make their greatest contribution. If they participate fully in the care of the chronically ill, they may help the traditional medical services to adapt themselves more quickly to the new realities. At present the structure and philosophy of our health-care arrangements (and of contemporary medical education) continue to reflect an outdated concern with infectious illnesses, accidents, surgery, hospital admissions, and so on. In his lucid analysis of these trends, William Glazier[1] asserts that

the medical system . . . is able to meet with high efficiency the kind of medical problem that was dominant until about forty years ago, namely, infectious disease. It also deals effectively with episodes of acute illness and with accidents that call for advanced, hospital-based bio-medical knowledge and technology. The system is much less effective in delivering the kind of care that is more often needed today: primary (first-contact) care and the kind of care needed at a time when chronic illnesses predominate. They are the degenerative diseases associated with aging and the diseases that can be characterized as man-made because they are associated with such things as smoking and environmental contaminants. For these diseases medicine has few measures and not even much comfort.

He goes on to point out that, in 1900, six of the ten leading causes of death were directly or indirectly due to infectious processes. But by 1970, none of the ten major causes of death, other than those associated with influenza-pneumonia, involved infectious processes. The contemporary causes of death are chronic diseases, with cancer, heart disease and cerebrovascular lesions the major contributors. According to his calculations, of every 100 males born in the United States nowadays, eighty-three are likely to die eventually of a chronic disease; by contrast, the likelihood of dying from an infectious disease is now about six in 100. The changing role of infectious and chronic diseases is illustrated in Figure 1.

Infectious diseases generally strike the patient suddenly and last for a brief and predictable length of time. Chronic diseases, on the other hand, usually begin insidiously and last indefinitely. Medical education and the structure of our medical services are still geared to the acute disorders and are inadequate in the face of the chronic disorders. Our arrangements work well, for example, when an acutely ill patient needs to see the same doctor several times over a short period of time. But in chronic disease he or she will need to see a variety of doctors and other health workers over a long period. Attempts to make arrangements for this type of care produce confusion, failures of communication, and a lack of continuity of care for the patient.

As Glazier points out, very little is being done to improve training in the long-term management and the home care of the chronically sick. Instead medical education continues to place undue emphasis–and to attribute unduly high status – to the hospital care of acute illness and

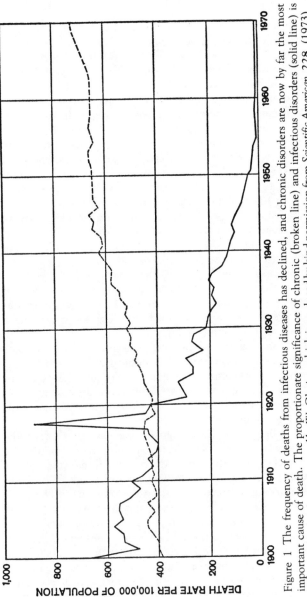

Figure 1 The frequency of deaths from infectious diseases has declined, and chronic disorders are now by far the most important cause of death. The proportionate significance of chronic (broken line) and infectious disorders (solid line) is illustrated in this figure prepared by W. Glazier, which is produced by kind permission from *Scientific American*, **228**, (1973).

injury. The imbalance is dramatically illustrated by the figures on medical training given by Fuchs.[2] As he points out: "The chief killers today are heart disease, cancer and violent deaths from accidents and homicide." Yet between 1950 and 1970 the number of surgical training posts in the United States more than doubled.

Psychologists should devote themselves to the majority of today's patients; those who cannot be helped by surgery or by episodic treatment. As Fuchs puts it: "the behavioral component in all these cases is very large, and until now medical care has not been very successful in altering behavior." Difficulty in altering the behavior of patients often prevents health-care workers from helping even those for whom medical technology has found solutions. For example, persistently elevated blood pressure (hypertension) is a major cause of both morbidity and mortality. The twenty-year mortality rate for hypertensive men between thirty-five and forty-five years of age is five times greater than that of a similar group with normal blood pressure readings, and they have a sixfold risk of suffering from congestive heart failure. Regular consumption of anti-hypertensive drugs substantially lowers these risks, yet studies have shown that less than half of the patients at risk carry out medical advice and take these drugs regularly (see Chapter 3). Medical technology has produced the drugs; doctors cannot persuade people at risk to take them. Here is a ready-made role for psychologists.

Pain control is another area where psychologists could make a major contribution. Melzack[3] has shown that psychological factors in the experience of pain and in its control are far more important where the pain is slowly rising and chronic than they are when it is acute but curtailed. Nowadays the most common pain complaints are of just this slow-rise, persistent type (see Chapter 4).

The increase in demand for health care has been described. Expenditure on health services cannot continue to expand at the rate of the past thirty years. We must establish limits to the continually growing calls for *professional* help before we reach the point at which one half of the population is devoting its time to treating the other half. The most obvious solution is to restore to people the major share in caring for their own health. This is an educational and psychological task of enormous magnitude but, in the long run, it will be easier and cheaper than risking the wholesale breakdown of a grossly overloaded health-care system. The move toward increased personal responsibility could be greatly facilitated by the abandonment of medical paternalism. Doctors, clinical psychologists, and other health workers must strive to be less secretive and coy, to set aside their verbal camouflage and learn how to advise rather than command. They must accept that the practice of medicine is not a private and privileged activity but one that involves many matters of public concern. Health care is financed by the community for the benefit of the community. The major say in the ordering of priorities and the allocation of resources, especially at the local level, should be returned by the medical profession to that community.

Physicians are accustomed to a large measure of independence and of executive control in the health-care services, but the era when the doctor was the sole medical care worker, meriting sole responsibility, is long over. In the United States, for example, there are 4.5 million health-care workers, of whom only 8 percent are physicians.[2] Doctors should acknowledge that their planning and executive powers greatly exceed their relative numbers, and that both power and responsibility must be dispersed. There is no doubt that priorities in the allocation of health-care resources would change if decision making became more broadly based.

Our first example is taken from an enlightening monograph on effectiveness and efficiency in the health services published by Dr. A. Cochrane,[4] Director of the British Medical Research Council Epidemiology Unit, in 1972. One of his examples is entitled "Two aspects of the ENT (ear nose and throat) world." He starts with the fact that the removal of tonsils is the commonest cause of admission of children to hospital, and argues convincingly that there is little evidence to support the present widespread use of this operation (see also Chapter 11). Cochrane says that

the present situation is therefore very unsatisfactory. . . . At present there seems every reason to limit tonsillectomy to cases of obstruction. No case should be placed on a surgical waiting-list, but always referred for medical treatment, and only when this fails after a prolonged trial should the case be sent to the surgeon. This should reduce the number of tonsillectomies to about one-third of the present numbers [p. 61].

Cochrane then goes on to contrast the "exuberant surgery discussed in the last section" with the service provided "by the *same ENT Departments* for the elderly deaf" (italics inserted). Very large numbers of people are affected by a loss of hearing capacity. In some surveys it was found that nearly one person in five had a significant hearing loss. According to Cochranes's estimates, there are "nearly a million old people with untreated hearing problems." He concludes his comparison by saying that here we have two types of therapy "which are probably effective in limited spheres: the first (tonsillectomy) is probably effective for only a small percentage of the cases operated on at present and has a definite mortality but it is an urgent dramatic therapy and is still rather fashionable" (p. 63). On the other hand, the service for people with hearing deficits, "while probably effective in improving the quality of life in some of a defined group of the population, is dull, smacks of a local authority service, is not nearly as fashionable, and serves the elderly. The first is applied inefficiently because it is too widely applied; the latter is applied inefficiently because it is under applied" (p. 63).

Despite the excellent progress made in health care for children, some outdated concepts and unnecessarily distressing practices persist. In the example we have chosen, the care of children in hospitals, many progressive changes have resulted in Britain from the work carried out by nonprofessional groups such as the National Association for the Welfare of Children in Hospital (NAWCH). In spite of the recommendations contained in the report of the Platt Commission on the care of children in hospitals, Stacey[5] and her colleagues found that many children's wards are still run in an authoritarian fashion, with many restrictions on parental visiting. In some wards, free parental visiting was encouraged in theory and effectively restricted in practice, even though the limited psychological evidence available indicates the value of flexible parental visiting, as opposed to confining and isolating children during the stress of their experience in the hospital (see Chapter 11). Medical and nursing staff have virtually uncontained power to operate undesirably restrictive ward systems, and the perpetuation of these practices is a matter for public concern. As we hope to demonstrate in Chapter 11, psychologists have already made a small but valuable contribution to improving the hospital care of children.

An unpleasant recent example of medical paternalism concerns the artificial induction of labor. This method of delivery was widely and uncritically adopted in the face of unpopularity among patients, partly for misguided medical reasons and partly for the convenience of hospital staff. To our knowledge, the objections and questions raised by pregnant women were often dismissed in a patronizing doctor-knows-best manner, notwithstanding the evidence that artificial inductions can introduce serious risks.

There are indications that these inductions increase the severity of contractions, raise the risks of fetal distress, jaundice, post-partum hemorrhages, and other complications.[6,7] In an editorial on the subject in 1974, the *Lancet*[7] reported that artificial induction "has become very common," and then put the question–"Is this sound clinical practice or meddlesome midwifery?" While recognizing that there are a few conditions in which artificial induction is medically necessary, they drew attention to the "mounting evidence" of the risks involved–"the main dangers are to the child itself." These dangers seem rarely to have been mentioned by medical teams trying to persuade (or more often simply "prescribing") mothers to have their labor started by artifical means. The *Lancet* urged that medical teams should

communicate their intentions and the reasons for these intentions to the patient–that the grounds for interference have taken into account the dangers of delivering or not delivering the child. Induction on the grounds of social or medical convenience is in a different category. Here, the clinician can no longer safely rely on his background of technical skill and knowledge to persuade or bemuse the patient. Anyone is free to join the argument . . . and it must be said at once . . . that induction on the grounds of social convenience is a pernicious practice.

In at least one leading London hospital, the staff repeatedly and strongly advised expectant mothers attending prenatal clinics to agree to artificia inductions weeks or even months in advance of the expected birth.

Despite the recent reappraisal carried out by one of the pioneers of the method, Professor Turnbull, it is still widely used. According to *The (London) Times* [8] (June 30, 1976), Turnbull now believes that "at present the clinical need is to go back to the spontaneous onset of labour instead of leaping to induce a baby because there were some grounds for concern. The spontaneous onset of labour is a robust and effective mechanism which is preceded by the maturation of several foetal systems. It should be given every opportunity to work on its own, unless it is certain that induction would be better." The induction rate at Oxford (his own university) has declined steadily from 56 percent in 1974 to 25 percent in 1976. At the same conference another professor of obstetrics, O'Driscoll of Dublin University, was reported as having said that

the induction technique had called into question a whole range of medical interventions during pregnancy and labour. It was essential to restore public confidence, either by presenting convincing evidence that a high rate of intervention was justified by improved results or by restricting the technique to patients who really needed it. . . . Three studies at Cardiff, Oxford and Dublin did not support the contention that induction had an important role in reducing perinatal mortality. The opposite might be true.

In this, as in other examples, unnecessary distress could have been avoided by greater candor–and, one might add, by better informed and more critical doctors.

The wasteful and often harmful excesses of medical prescribing are discussed in Chapter 7, but some recent estimates reported by the medical correspondent of the *New Scientist*, Donald Gould,[9] are worth mentioning here. It is estimated that "more than half the adult population of Britain, and almost one-third of all children, take some kind of medication every day." Moreover, some 75 percent of all medicines swallowed are obtained on repeat prescriptions. The seriousness of this epidemic of pill taking is underlined by the estimate that at least 30 percent of hospital patients suffer from "some kind of unwanted effect from the drugs they take, and in 5 percent of hospital admissions a drug has contributed to the condition" that brought the patient into hospital in the first place.

The poor communication between patients and doctors is a large and important subject and is dealt with at some length in Chapter 3. Here we shall mention only the evidence of a major disagreement between patients and doctors. It appears that despite the wishes of a large majority of their patients, most doctors are extremely reluctant to be frank about serious illnesses. Some of the reasons for this disagreement and possible solutions are considered in Chapter 3.

To the extent that medicine is a public concern, the arguments and proposals contained in this book are of public interest. As far as professional groups are concerned, we hope that the arguments and proposals will be considered not merely by psychologists and doctors, but by nurses-for whom many of these notions may be of considerable importance in conducting their work, and especially in facilitating change from a passive helping role to a more therapeutic function. We hope that occupational and physiotherapists, social workers (especially medical and psychiatric social workers), and health administrators (now one of the largest and most important of the new professions) will also find parts of this book of direct interest.

2 Psychology and behavioral medicine

Within the medical profession there is a growing appreciation of the importance of psychological factors in what is sometimes called the "process of becoming ill." It is also agreed that psychological factors contribute to the process of recovery. Unfortunately, psychologists have been slow to recognize and respond to the need for a psychological approach to problems of illness and health, outside psychiatry. One purpose of this book is to present a case for widening the scope of clinical psychology to include medical problems as well as those of a psychiatric character. We feel that the expansion is feasible as well as desirable, and illustrate our general theme with examples from the psychology of pain, sleep disturbances, placebos, and pill taking, among others.

As mentioned in Chapter 1, the great advances in medical knowledge registered over the last fifty years have not led to the declining need for medical services predicted by social reformers. Illnesses such as tuberculosis, diphtheria, and pneumonia, which formerly resulted in premature deaths, have been controlled, and many serious and handicapping illnesses of former years are now managed well enough to allow people to live a full life. Over the same period, however, we have seen a greater number of referrals and admissions to hospitals, a growing demand for medical investigations and even larger increases in prescriptions and rates of absence because of sickness. The paradox is neatly expressed in a publication of the British Office of Health Economics (OHE), *Medicine and Society:* "While the population in absolute terms has clearly become healthier, it is nevertheless seeking and receiving very much more medical treatment."[1] The control of the most serious illnesses has been followed by an increase in requests for medical assistance in coping with other problems, discomforts, and minor illnesses.

[The public] perceive and act on symptoms which previously they would have ignored. Discomforts which they would have considered irrelevant in the days when premature death and crippling disability from serious disease were commonplace are now thought to justify medical treatment.

As a result, far more attention is being paid to the psychological and social elements in medical services. "It is realized that much more understanding is needed of the non-medical factors affecting demands for treatment." The Office of Health Economics publication points out that the "naive assumption" that a state of illness is easily defined or easily recognized is "no longer valid." It seems that most people feel unwell very frequently (in one London survey, 95 percent of the respondents had experienced some symptoms during the previous two weeks), and we also know that only a small minority of people consult a doctor when they experience minor symptoms. For the most part, people take self-prescribed remedies on these occasions. A small number of cases are also identifiable in which, despite the presence of serious illness, the potential patient does not recognize or perhaps admit the presence of illness. Others consult their doctors for trivial reasons. The first definition of the presence of illness is made by the person affected, usually in conjunction with close relatives. It is not, in the first instance, a medical decision. Recent information has also shown that tolerance for minor discomforts and distress varies in members of different groups. In one industrial study, it was possible to distinguish between employees who were frequently sick and those who were rarely sick. People who were dissatisfied with their jobs, or had family troubles, or unstable personalities, were absent through sickness three times more often than a comparison group of stable people. In another context, it was found that the main determinant of whether or not a child was sent to a guidance clinic for medical consultation was the mother's attitude to the child and the problem.[2] The OHE report points out that "an increasing proportion of the workload in general practice concerns social and psychological problems rather than physical ones." The report goes on: "The needs which people are expressing when they consult their doctor as a reaction to their social (or psychological) situation are very real, even if they are not medical in the traditional sense." It is argued that if the medical profession is to accept these, education will "need to be even further broadened" into the related disciplines of psychology and sociology. "The medical school must in the future also concentrate more on teaching general practitioners about human behavior, rather than merely extending their technical medical knowledge."

Steps toward a medical psychology

Psychologists failed to respond to these important psychological changes in general medical care because of their almost exclusive concern with psychiatric problems. Bearing in mind the fact that psychology is the study of behavior and experience, one can no longer see any reason why applied psychology should be restricted to psychiatric abnormalities, nor is there any satisfactory reason for clinical psychologists to ignore or avoid the vast number of behavioral problems that arise in all aspects of health services. In this book, we introduce and consider some new possibilities that an enlargement of the scope of psychology would offer. We have not attempted to produce a detailed or systematic exposition of these possibilities but, rather, to introduce ideas. In some of the chapters we give a methodical account of one subject, such as pain, whereas in other chapters we provide a bird's-eye view of the subject supplemented by concrete proposals and recommendations.

At present the term "medical psychology" is taken to mean something close to psychiatric psychology. There is no reason for retaining this exceedingly narrow definition; "medical psychology" should refer to *all* the applications of normal and abnormal psychology to medicine.

We are advocating no less than a fundamental change in the scope of clinical psychology. Many psychologists have started on the work of reappraising their discipline, some belatedly[3] and other presciently,[4-6] but almost all of them with optimism. Most psychologists welcome the expansion and, if it is successful, they will have to deal with fresh intellectual problems and develop new skills.

It is legitimate to ask, however, what the medical profession can expect to gain. In the first place, they would receive additional assistance in dealing with certain types of clinical problem. In the longer run, the theory of medicine might be enriched and the practice of medicine regain some lost interest and personal rewards. The infusion of psychology might also help to smoothe the inevitable transition from paternalistic medicine to newer forms. It could help doctors to establish more satisfactory personal relationships with their patients and to develop their important educational functions. Patients, in turn, would be encouraged to become less dependent on their doctors and to play an active part in maintaining their own health.

One cannot argue with history. To a large extent clinical psychology grew up in the shadow of psychiatry. There is little doubt that this relationship was mutually beneficial, despite the unnecessary limitations that were placed on psychologists. Having acquired considerable knowledge about abnormal behavior and expertise in its assessment and modification, it would be foolish to abandon the application of psychology to psychiatric problems (see Chapter 10).

Some of the applications of psychology that we shall discuss have already been the subject of clinical work and research, whereas, others are speculative. We discuss the potential and actual psychological contributions to problems of pain, sleep disorders, pill taking, hospital admissions, doctor–patient relationships, failure to comply with medical advice, smoking, obesity, headaches, cardiac disorders, psychiatric disturbances, and some psychosomatic disorders. There are many other common problems that are not taken up here at any length; among them are child development, sexual disorders, and speech disorders.

Child psychology is one of the best-developed specialties within the discipline, but so far it has made little impact on medical care, despite the fact that infant and child welfare services are such a valuable part of modern health services. Advice on child care is provided on a large scale, usually by nursing staff. Although much of it, born of many years of experience, appears to be useful and desirable, there is no doubt that child psychologists already are in a position to extend and improve these services. Their contribution could be made quickly and usefully. If the opportunity is taken, it should be possible in a few years' time to place the advice given to parents on a more scientific basis; to write a psychologist's version of Spock. The work of Patterson is a first step in this direction.[7,8] Although Spock's reassuring tone is as invaluable as his pediatric advice, his ventures into child psychology are remarkably uncritical.

A subject of immediate medical and nursing concern is the psychological effect of admission to a hospital, and other occasions of separation of a child from his or her parents. The growth of knowledge about normal child development has already helped to clarify a number of the common problems of childhood, including eating and elimination difficulties.[9] Advances in operant conditioning, a type of reward training, are giving rise to a new technology which is already being introduced into clinical child psychology.[7]

As we shall see, a useful start has also been made in attempting to understand the psychological consequences of various types of medical procedures. The recent advances in psycholinguistics, the study of language development and functions, are likely in the future to be relevant in the management of speech disorders, and advances in behavioral genetics are of wider significance.

The effects of active and inert drugs have been investigated extensively within a psychiatric setting by psychologists, and for this reason it is not so much a new departure as an extension into other branches of medicine. The subject of pain is another with which psychologists are already acquainted. As it is a major source of discomfort and complaint among people requesting assistance from the health services, it is reasonable that psychologists should be asked to put greater effort into understanding the nature of pain and its modification–and not simply within psychiatric samples. A related but more specific problem arises in the practice of surgery, where we have a great deal to learn about how patients can best be prepared for operations and, even more challenging, how they can best be assisted to make rapid and satisfactory recovery. The problems of dental care, especially in the young, have concerned dentists and educators for a long time, but have attracted few psychologists. It should be possible to develop improved training techniques to ensure that children learn hygienic habits of care of the teeth and prevention of disease. In addition, some of the fear-reduction techniques already used by psychologists have an important part to play in reducing or eliminating the anxiety and distress often involved in dental treatment (see Chapter 10).

Group techniques

A second, but lesser development that we would like to encourage is a shift of emphasis from individual casework to the refinement and implementation of group techniques. This change is needed because of the multiplicity of problems that will require attention and the certainty that we shall never have sufficient numbers of qualified psychologists to deal with them as long as the present style of concentrating on individual patients is retained. The impossibility of confining almost all their clinical work to individual patients will become increasingly apparent as the scope of psychology is expanded. It is not suggested that individual casework should be abandoned, but rather that an exclusive concern with individual work will lead to an unrealistic situation in which psychologists are doing more and more work for fewer and fewer people until they are reduced to working with an infinitesimal proportion of the population. There are two ways in which the size of their clinical contribution can be enlarged. Firstly, techniques of group management can be developed and administered. For example, it should be possible to develop procedures designed to suppress or prevent pain, and, once available, these could be taught to several people at the same time. Or to take a psychiatric example, the introduction of a token economy system (a reward training method) on a psychiatric ward enables one to provide assistance for twenty to forty patients within the same treatment program.

A second, general, way in which the contribution of psychologists can be spread to a larger population is through the execution of problem-solving research, the fruits of which can be handed over to members of ancillary professions to administer. For example, if psychologists were able to develop techniques for improving habits of dental hygiene among children, these findings could be passed on to dentists, school doctors, health visitors, nurses, and so on.

When the two main proposals advocated here, enlarging the scope of psychology and placing greater emphasis on group work, are adopted, a sequence of changes will result. The theory of clinical psychology will have to be expanded to include the application of psychological science to behavioral problems that arise in psychologically normal people who have general medical problems. This change in orientation has many practical consequences. First, the training and preparation of psychologists must be altered to give them a more general clinical education. It also follows that although a minority of clinical psychologists will continue to work in psychiatric settings, the majority will be employed in hospitals, community health centers, social service departments, and allied agencies. Current clinical practice, which concentrates on assessments based on standardized psychological tests, counseling, and modification of abnormal behavior will develop into new shapes. The relative importance of psychometric test assessments is diminishing, whereas counseling and modification techniques are being extended beyond the field of abnormal behavior. Two types of undertaking are becoming increasingly important: the establishment of new systems of guidance and care within the health services, and the development of trouble-shooting psychologists who can be called into any part of the hospital or health services whenever a behavioral difficulty is proving to be an obstacle to the administration and acceptance of required or desired treatment or prevention plans (for example, failures of diabetic patients to give themselves insulin injections). The scope of psychological research will have to be expanded, and psychologists will need to display some boldness in entering uncharted waters. Perhaps the first and essential step is to change our view of what constitutes a psychological problem. We are convinced that a few months spent wandering around a general hospital or in general practice would produce a profusion of research problems for any psychologist.

3 Doctor's orders

Research has shown that the majority of patients express overall satisfaction with the medical care they receive, in or out of the hospital.[1,2] A significant minority expresses some dissatisfaction, and one of their major complaints concerns failures of communication: Patients feel that doctors fail to supply them with adequate information about their condition and its management.

Doctors most commonly express discontent about the failure of their patients to carry out the advice or treatment recommended. There can be few doctors who are at a loss for spectacular examples of patients who do not comply with their instructions – diabetics who forget to take their insulin and thereby risk death, hypertensive patients who risk heart failure by neglecting to take their (effective) drugs, bronchitic patients who continue to smoke. It is when doctors are dismayed by this apparently inexplicable behavior that the psychologists' task begins. As yet, they have little to offer in the way of direct advice, but they do possess a theory and methodology for studying human behavior that enables them to undertake the task. As we shall see, there is evidence that patient cooperation is enhanced by a good personal relationship with the doctor (and, in any event, for most doctors this is a basic belief). Psychologists can explore ways of establishing and maintaining satisfying and effective patient-doctor relationships. Attention should also be paid to the nature and causes of poor relationships, with a view to improving them. In this chapter we shall examine selected aspects of the relation between doctor and patient (including communications) from a mainly psychological point of view, discuss some proposed remedies, and suggest some lines of development.

There is evidence that many patients are unable to recall the greater part of what their doctor tells them in their consultation, within minutes of seeing him or her. In one study it was found that within five minutes, patients had forgotten 50 percent of what the doctor had told them during the consultation.[3] As a result of this poor retention, many patients fail to act on the doctor's advice. One of us had a vivid demonstration of this disarming fact a few years ago when he was a patient in a surgical ward. Each evening the medication cart was rolled into the ward by at least two nurses, who carefully supervised the correct allocation of drugs to each patient. They went to great lengths to check and countercheck the delivery of each pill, which was meticulously recorded in a duty book. For the most part the patients accepted the medicine with apparent gratitude. Shortly after the nurses had trundled their cart along to the next ward, many of the patients who were able to get up – usually at least half the number on the ward – would retire to the bathrooms and surreptitiously or ceremoniously, depending on individual styles, flush the medication down the lavatory.

It has not come as a total surprise, therefore, to learn from Ley that 48.7 percent of patients fail to take their antibiotics, 37.5 percent fail to take their antituberculosis drugs, and so on.[2,3] To make matters worse, some studies of outpatients have shown that even among those patients who attempt to adhere to their doctor's advice, anything from one-quarter to two-thirds may be taking the wrong dose, and up to 30 percent are making errors that are potentially dangerous.

Another, more poignant example of the barriers that sometimes exist between doctor and patient is described by Fletcher, who quotes a colleague as estimating that "80 percent of dying patients know that they are dying and would wish to talk about it and 80 percent of doctors deny this and believe that patients should not be told" (p. 29).[4] This estimate is consistent with the few available attitude surveys, from which it emerges that members of the medical profession generally are of the opinion that most patients do not wish to be told if and when they have a fatal condition. Patients, on the other hand, express a desire to be told the worst. It appears that the argument for keeping patients in ignorance, on the grounds that they only wish to hear good news, may be unfounded. Aitken-Swan and Easson, for example, informed 231 of their patients when they had cancer, and only 7 percent of them subsequently said that they would rather not have known.[5] This important and extremely sensitive subject calls for full and careful psychological research.

In one survey, no less than two-thirds of discharged patients expressed dissatisfaction with the communications of the hospital. In other surveys, including some carried out in well-staffed teaching hospitals, this proportion was slightly lower (between 30 percent and 60 percent) but still unacceptably high. Ley and Spelman point out that dissatisfaction with communications (usually complaints of receiving inadequate information about their problems and treatment) is the most frequent criticism made by patients.[6,7] They add that improved communications can reduce stress and improve patient's contributions to their own treatment, for instance, by keeping to the prescribed diet, carrying out required exercises, actually taking pills prescribed, and so on. It has been suggested that a major reason for this dissatisfaction is the decline of the traditional system of medicine, which centered on the establishment of a familiar and trusting relationship with a single family doctor.[1] As this system is replaced by short consultations with unfamiliar doctors, the opportunity for establishing such a relationship is precluded. In the shift from a familiar and comforting figure to a higly trained and technically more competent specialist in medicine, we are in danger of overlooking the considerable part played by psychological factors in ensuring accurate and satisfactory communications between doctor and patient, and, as a by-product of this communication, satisfactory compliance with the pre-scribed course of action. In his review of 68 studies, Ley[3] found that, on average, slightly more than half of the patients acted on their doctor's advice. Very many patients ignored advice even when it was vital for their health.

In an attempt to come to grips with some aspects of the communica-tion between doctor and patient and its relation to the successful practice of medicine, Korsch and Negrete[1] have been conducting valuable re-search at a children's hospital in Los Angeles. The greatest part of their research has been carried out in an emergency pediatric clinic staffed by highly trained young doctors with between one and three years of pediat-ric experience. The visits are usually short and generally result in a specific recommendation from the doctor to the parent. The usual reason for the emergency visit is an acute but generally minor illness. In their major study they observed the visits of 800 different patients (i.e., parent and child), and interviewed the mother in each case. Most of the inter-views were tape recorded; the mother was questioned immediately after each consultation and then again fourteen days later to ascertain if she had carried out the doctor's advice. The information from this major study was supplemented by observations made in general practice, well-baby clinics, and the like.

The most reassuring finding to emerge from the major study was that three-quarters of the mothers were satisfied with the doctors' perfor-mance in their brief consultation. Despite this general satisfaction, how-ever, there are grounds for concern, as nearly half the mothers were unclear about what had caused their child's illness. The importance of this finding is that many of the mothers assumed incorrectly that they might have been negligent, and this was an unnecessary source of distress for them. Moreover, only 42 percent of the mothers carried out all the doctor's advice, 11 percent did not comply at all, and one-third carried out part of the instructions only (data were unobtainable for the remain-ing 14 percent). As might be expected, there was a close association between the mother's satisfaction with the consultation and the extent to which she carried out the doctor's advice. Rather surprisingly, how-ever, there was no correlation between the duration of the consultation and the amount of satisfaction expressed by the mother, or between the duration of the consultation and the clarity of the diagnosis offered to the mother.

Among the specific complaints leveled by the mothers was a lack of interest shown by the doctor, the excessive use of jargon which was often misunderstood (for instance, "lumbar puncture" gave rise to misunderstandings), and a lack of empathy with the anxious mothers. It was also found that the doctors talked more than the mothers and that only 5 percent of the doctor's conversation was personal or friendly. The main findings of Korsch and Negrete can be summarized:

> Friendly treatment of the patient (e.g., the mother) generally had favorable results: harsh treatment tended to yield poor results. And there was a direct statistical relation between the amount of non-medical (that is, sociable) conversation between doctor and patient and the patient's satisfaction with the encounter with the doctor [p. 74].[1]

The importance of these findings is twofold. In the first place, they show how easy it is to provide comfort for the anxious mother of a sick child and, equally, how easy it is to ignore this most obvious need. Second, these research workers were able to demonstrate a close relationship between the mother's satisfaction with the consultation and the extent to which she carried out prescribed treatment.

We shall give one closing observation from this study. As the quotation above shows, the friendliness expressed by the doctor made a valuable contribution to the mother's satisfaction. Most of the doctors believed that they had been friendly, but less than half of the patients shared this impression! It is on differences of perception and impression such as these that deep and lasting misunderstandings are built and sustained.

In those studies where checks have been carried out (by laboratory tests, the use of external informants, and so on), it is found that patients ignore a surprising amount of medical advice. For example, in a study quoted by Ley and Spelman, no fewer than twenty-seven out of fifty diabetic patients failed to take their prescribed insulin regularly and correctly.[6] The finding that up to 50 percent of patients may fail to take their prescribed drugs has also been reported for ulcer patients, psychiatric patients (failure to take drugs is a major cause of relapse in schizophrenia), and other groups. Furthermore, general advice such as the use of diets, relaxation classes, vitamins for babies, and so on, has been reported to be followed by fewer than half the patients concerned. In a treatment study of the effects of a psychological method on the occurrence of bed wetting at night among children living in a poor area, no fewer than thirty-nine out of eighty-one mothers failed to carry out the necessary procedures.[7] This disappointingly high failure rate occurred despite the deliberate exclusion from treatment of children whose parents seemed on first interview to be unable or unwilling to comply with the requirements of the treatment regime, and despite our provision of a full explanation and demonstration of what was required. It is interesting to note that the failure of parents to carry out the treatment program was significantly reduced when the children concerned were given tablets to take. The parental failure rate in cases where tablets were not given was 30 percent, but only 12 percent with a stimulant tablet.

The treatment of hypertension (persistently elevated blood pressure levels) is an excellent current example of the need for improved psychological understanding and skill. As mentioned earlier, hypertension is a serious chronic condition. Drugs capable of significantly reducing hypertension, and hence of reducing the risks to health and life, are now available, but large numbers of the people affected appear to be reluctant to continue taking maintenance drugs for prolonged periods. In common with other similar studies, the project carried out by Sackett[8] and his colleagues revealed a very large noncooperation rate. Almost 50 percent of their sample of 230 hypertensive patients failed to take their tablets for longer than six months, despite the provision of special health instruction courses and well-organized, convenient medical supervision. In a second, more intensive study[9] of a subsample of thirty-eight of these noncompliant patients, some progress was made. When the patients were given greater responsibility for monitoring their own progress, and sessions with the supervisor of their regimes were held every two weeks, the adherance rate increased by 21 percent. Among the twenty patients who carried out the regime satisfactorily, seventeen achieved a reduction in blood pressure. The scope for improving the psychological aspects of this treatment is extensive; our own expectation is that the social influences on the patient, especially from relatives and friends, will prove to be particularly powerful determinants of adherence to prescribed programs of self-care.

Like earlier investigators, Ley and Spelman found evidence of misconceptions about medical matters in a lay population, but they were rather less extensive and serious than might have been feared.[6] Certainly, lay knowledge was greater than predicted by a sample of doctors – in one study it was shown that 81 percent of a sample of doctors underestimated their patients' knowledge. Moreover, the doctors were inclined to give the least information to their worst-informed patients.

Assessing how much of the information and advice given by doctors was recalled by their patients, Ley and Spelman found that a good deal, roughly one-third, was forgotten promptly. Fortunately, the most important bits of information were generally the best recalled. Notable exceptions have been encountered, however, in which patients forgot the diagnosis, even of a serious illness, within a few weeks of being informed. The same workers have also found that patients who have a good knowledge of medical matters recall better than ignorant ones, and an anxious patient finds it more difficult to recall the doctor's information and advice. On the other hand, neither age nor intelligence was related to the degree of forgetfulness. Another interesting finding, which would bear considerable development, is that patients' satisfaction varies with their moods. It was found that when there was little depression (upon discharge from the hospital), satisfaction was fairly high. When the patient become more depressed between two and four weeks after discharge, satisfaction correspondingly declined. Lastly, when depression lessened again in the eighth week, satisfaction once again increased.

Ley and his colleagues have not been content with mere identification and description of inadequate communication, but have also attempted to improve the quality and durability of the communications. Some of their preliminary findings suggest that the patient could more accurately recall the doctor's information if the doctor gave the most important information first and emphasized the few most important aspects of it.[10] Recall was also made easier when the doctor presented the information in a logical sequence – for instance, "This is what is wrong with you, this is what we will do, this is what will happen, this is what treatment you need, and this is what you must do to help yourself." They have also found that extra visits by the doctor increased the patient's understanding and, ultimately, compliance.

Other suggestions that might be worth taking up include the use of memory aids in the form of written material, as well as, or instead of, conveying the essential information to at least one other person, such as a close relative. From the research of Korsch and Negrete in California, the lesson seems to be that we need to assist doctors in achieving a friendly manner which will increase the satisfaction of the patient and thereby improve compliance. There is considerable psychological literature on the persuasive effects of various forms of communication, briefly described later, that can be used in improving doctor–patient and patient–doctor interactions.

Communicating with doctors

So far attention has been paid almost exclusively to the failure of doctors to communicate adequately with their patients. This attention is not misplaced because, as we have already seen, this is the most common complaint leveled by patients at the medical care they receive. This should not, however, obscure the failures of communication in other direction–that is, from patient to doctor. There is some evidence that failure of communication underlies the most common complaint reported by the *doctors*. As we have seen, they feel that far too many of their patients fail to cooperate in carrying out the advice and instructions given to them. In our view there is another important cause of dissatisfaction among doctors that seems so far to have escaped attention.

Most psychologists would agree that the consequences of a particular form of behavior play a major part in determining if the behavior will be modified. If the consequences of behavior are unknown, obscure, or infrequently observed, it is far less likely that the behavior will change. This can be stated more positively: The provision of prompt and accurate information about the consequences of our behavior will facilitate learning and improvements. In many circumstances, particularly general practice, feedback of this type is, at best, irregularly provided. Doctors in general practice seldom see the best results of their work, as the patients who recover or are otherwise satisfied are *not* the ones who return for further consultations. This means that for the most part general practitioners receive little reward for their efforts; they have to deduce from the fact that their patients do not turn up again in the waiting room that their advice or treatment has been successful. On the other hand, the failure of a course of treatment is more likely to be brought to their notice. In other words, doctors receive frequent reminders of failure and infrequent acknowledgments of success. It seem likely to us that this situation will produce adverse results, as it is bound to be demoralizing for many doctors. If a psychologist set out deliberately to design a program of persistent punishment, he or she would need to add little to the existing system under which most general practitioners function.

In addition to the emotional effects of exposure to a punishment "learning" situation of this type, the erratic and unbalanced flow of information coming back to doctors from their patients provides ideal conditions for inducing behavioral changes of the wrong type. Successful actions on the doctor's part are rarely and irregularly reinforced. Ineffective actions, on the other hand are regularly "punished" (by the repeated returns of the dissatisfied patients), and the doctor can only hope that the fact that a patient does not return means that he or she is cured. As we know, however, a high proportion of patients who feel dissatisfied with a particular piece of advice or recommended treatment will avoid telling their doctors. Instead they go elsewhere, try self-medication, or seek nonmedical assistance.

In this muddled situation the doctor's dilemma can be put in this way: If a patient fails to return for a second consultation after a course of therapeutic action has been prescribed, one of three conclusions is possible: The therapy may have been effective and there is therefore no need for the patient to return; the therapy may have been ineffective but the patient does not request a second consultation because he or she has sought help elsewhere; or the patient did not act on the advice anyway – either because he failed to understand the instruction or because, understanding it, he decided not to carry out the doctor's suggestion.

Let us translate this into a hypothetical example of a general practitioner who, in the course of one month, is consulted by ten patients suffering from stomach ulcers. In each of the ten cases the doctor recommends that a prescribed drug be taken three times daily and, in addition, that the patient keep to a special diet, the details of which are provided. Within a month three of the patients return to complain that they have had no relief. How is this outcome to be interpreted? Does it mean that the course of treatment recommended is effective in the majority of cases? Strictly speaking, all that the doctor could conclude is that it is ineffective in a minority of cases and has unknown effects in the majority of cases.

The seven patients who do not seek a second consultation may have derived considerable benefit from the treatment, or they may have sought help elsewhere, or they may have decided not to take the pills nor to keep to the prescribed diet. It is easy to see how a general practitioner forced to rely solely on his or her own clinical experience would be compelled to make decisions on the basis of "systematic chaos." Fortunately for everyone concerned, this is not the only source of information available to doctors. The position is, and it will certainly remain so in the future, that they have recourse to information obtained in other settings, in a systematic and controlled manner.

It is easy, however, to think of simple expedients to improve the flow of information back to the doctor. Although some of the problems seem to be almost insurmountable (such as ascertaining the reliability of some of the information), the introduction of a regular feedback system by means of telephone calls, postcards, or reports from health visitors would be a useful improvement. For obvious reasons the return flow of information is greater in most hospitals (for instance, the opportunity for repeated and prolonged observations), but even here a substantial amount of valuable psychological information is lost – simply for the lack of trying.

We look forward to psychological investigations designed to improve the flow of information to doctors and to assess the effect of this information on their level of satisfaction and effectiveness.

Persuasive communications

Although there are endless stories about patients, even seriously ill ones, who ignore the clear warnings given to them by their doctors, there is some encouraging evidence to show that a well-timed and forceful piece of advice from a GP can be extremely effective. To take one example, Williams states that roughly 37 percent of patients with chest complaints gave up smoking when strongly advised to do so by their medical practitioner.[11] As far as we can tell at present, many people do respond to warnings about their health. We also know that in many circumstances a more alarming message is more effective in changing people's attitudes. Unfortunately, changes of attitude obtained in this way do not necessarily lead to action. When even messages that arouse considerable fear fail to persuade, it often means that the recipient is unable to take appropriate action. The best combination seems to be a fear-evoking message followed by instructions that make it easier for the appropriate action to be taken. For example, Leventhal found that one in three of his subjects took an antitetanus shot after receiving a fear-provoking warning combined with specific action instructions that were easy to carry out. When the action instructions were omitted, however, only one person in thirty took the appropriate steps.[12]

In an influential early study of this topic it was found that a low-fear message was more effective than a high-fear message.[13] School children were first instructed in dental care and then given either high, low, or moderate fear-provoking information about the dangers of inadequate dental care. The pupils who received a high-fear message showed least improvement in caring for their teeth. For some time psychologists thought that this apparent greater effectiveness of low-fear messages might be generally the case. Later findings have shown, however, that in many instances a high-fear message is in fact more effective - at the very least, for changing attitudes, if not always for inducing a change in behavior. For example, Leventhal and his colleagues reported some success in using a fear-provoking film of an operation to remove lung cancer in changing the attitudes of a group of smokers.[14] They also observed a slight tendency for patients who saw this film to act on the recommendation that, as smokers, they should take advantage for the easy facilities for obtaining a chest X-ray. In a second group of smokers who received similar background information to the first two groups but did not see the film showed less attitude change, and fewer of them took advantage of the X-ray service. So, in this instance at least, a fear-provoking appeal brought about the desired change in attitude and, to a lesser degree, the desired action.

In this study there was a weak relationship between the change in attitude and effective action. This poor correspondence between attitude change and behavioral change has been reported on a number of occasions.[15] Even when high-fear-provoking messages are more successful in changing attitudes, it has been found that considerably less alarming messages are just as successful in producing changes in *behavior*. So, for example, it has been found that alarming messages about the dangers of smoking produce greater changes in attitude; but, despite this, the reduction in actual smoking is similar for groups receiving messages that provoke high or low levels of fear. Similar findings have been reported by psychologists attempting to persuade people to take antitetanus injections. Despite the more favorable attitudes induced by fear-provoking messages, there was no difference between the high- or low-fear groups in the numbers of those who obtained the injection.

It should be remembered that frightening messages can be ineffective. It has been suggested that in medical matters a failure to act on the advice given in an alarming message may arise from the possibility that the action proposed is itself painful or distressing. So, heavy smokers may fail to undergo the recommended X-ray because they are aware that a positive finding might lead to chest surgery; a positive X-ray diagnosis of tuberculosis may lead to protracted treatment in a hospital, and so on.

Psychologists are also beginning to show an interest in individual differences in response to health-care messages. For instance, it seems likely that people with low self-esteem may be less likely to act on recommended diagnostic or treatment procedures, particularly if frightening messages are used. Fear-producing warnings may reinforce their sense of hopelessness and the belief that the dangers cannot successfully be avoided. For people with low self-esteem it may be preferable to use messages that produce little fear and contain clear, specific, simple instructions for taking appropriate action. Let us take a hypothetical example. Among sufferers from venereal disease, those who have low self-esteem will be more likely to seek treatment if given an only mildly fearful warning coupled with specific and simple advice about how and where to obtain treatment. Care should be taken to emphasize that the treatment is generally brief and painless, as it usually is. As recommendations for treatment have been shown to be more persuasive if they are described as being highly effective, it should also be pointed out to VD sufferers that current methods are in fact extremely successful.

The reluctance to transmit bad news

In the nature of their work, doctors, nurses, physiotherapists, occupational therapists, social workers, and psychologists are required to convey bad news to their patients or clients or to their relatives. It is often the case that the reluctance to transmit bad news is disguised by health workers, who attribute their own reluctance to the putative reluctance of the recipient of the news - the patient doesn't really want to know the worst.

In the last few years psychologists have made a modest start in studying the widespread reluctance to transmit bad news. In their thorough review of progress so far, Tesser and Rosen quote "numerous experiments that consistently demonstrate our reluctance to convey bad news."[16] In a variety of settings, using experimental situations that range from the extremely artificial to the realistic, psychologists have shown that people are indeed reluctant to transmit bad news, and that, given the option, they will refrain from doing so. Among some of the secondary findings, it is interesting to learn that we are more reluctant to convey bad news to emotional people than to calm people. This is related to the messenger's sense of his own competence to deal with the exceptional emotional reactions to the news; people who have little confidence in their ability to deal with the expected emotional reactions are more likely to have difficulty in conveying the news. On the other hand, people who are confident of their ability to deal with the emotional reactions show less reluctance to convey the news. As far as we are aware, teaching people how to convey bad news, how to deal with the effects of this news, does not feature in the training of doctors, nurses, psychologists, and so on . At the same time, it has been reported by Saul and Kass[17] that students starting medical studies anticipated that they would be most distressed by the need to discuss a fatal illness with a patient, and by the need to inform the relatives that a patient had died. In a reassessment carried out after the students had completed their first year of training, it turned out that they had correctly anticipated what would most distress them.

It is of course true that many of the skills such as conveying bad news are acquired informally, especially by modeling the behavior of effective and successful practitioners. However, there will be few people who contest the view that we need to know a great deal more about the subject of how to transmit bad news and how to deal with the effects, both short and long term, of such news. It follows that as our knowledge and understanding increase, teaching of these psychological skills will play a more important part in the formal and informal teaching of medical and other health professions. As yet, we know very little about the long-term effect of receiving seriously bad news about one's health. Apart from the obvious effects of such news (e.g., preparation for death, declining capacity), we are told that some patients with fatal illnesses are themselves reluctant to disseminate this news because they complain that people cease to behave naturally toward them once they learn of the illness. It is said that relatives and friends tend to become secretive and to regard people with fatal illnesses as being oversensitive and incapable of dealing with difficult or stressful subjects.

Although the research into the reluctance to transmit bad news is still in its very early stages, Tesser and Rosen discuss three possible explanations for this reluctance. In the first place, they suggest that people might be reluctant to convey bad news because it arouses guilt in them. A second possibility is that people fear that as messengers they will be tarnished by the bad news and that, as a consequence, people will value them less. A third possibility is that people are unwilling to convey bad news because it means that they have to adopt a negative emotional state in order to delivery the bad news–this is proposed on the reasonable grounds that one has to assume an appropriate emotional state before conveying bad news. It cannot be said, however, that any of these three explanations is satisfactory, and as Tesser and Rosen point out, none of them has received much support. There is another possibility, however, and it is one that they mention without developing. It seems to us that the reluctance to convey bad news might result from the fact that the observed effects of conveying bad news are inherently unpleasant. We can take it that, on the whole, observing a person in distress is inherently unpleasant for most people. We can also take it that, on the whole, people will make vigorous attempts to avoid exposing themselves to unpleasant events. Hence it follows that we are reluctant to convey bad news.

The belief held by many doctors that patients do not want to know the worst news, while almost certainly true for a small number of people, may be based more on the general reluctance we all have for transmitting bad news, and a confusion between the occurrence of the unfortunate event and informing the recipient of the fact. It is a confusion that serves a purpose and one can sympathize with it, even if it is difficult to defend in practice. We cannot refrain from speculating on the relations between this reluctance to transmit bad news, the growth of medical paternalism, and the establishment of medical hierarchies. Did this reluctance perhaps contribute to the distance that developed between doctors and their patients, and the elevation of medical euphemisms into a minor art form? Is the hierarchical organization of the profession a useful arrangement for passing on the responsibility for transmitting bad news?

Withholding the news from a person who has cancer does not modify the cancer. In many circumstances, if the person is adequately informed, he or she can begin to make the necessary psychological and other preparations for a chronic and possibly fatal illness. Improved psychological understanding of our reluctance to transmit bad news will lead to the development of methods for telling people the worst and for preparing them for the short- and long-term consequences implied by the news. In passing, it may be of some interest to mention that it is our impression, obtained from conversations with colleagues in varied professions, that nurses and clinical psychologists are particularly eager to obtain guidance on this subject.

As Ley[3] points out, what started as a humanitarian concern for candor and honesty has resulted in confirmation of the practical value of providing patients with information. "As it turns out, patients' satisfaction and their compliance with advice are related . . . the achievement of the humanitarian aim leads to the achievement of the practical one" (p. 9).

4 Pain

Despite the universality and impact of painful experiences, clinical psychologists have neglected the subject. Instead, many of them still spend much of their working lives puzzling over the mysteries of what their psychiatrically disturbed subjects perceive in inkblots. This imbalance, which is of course one of the less fortunate consequences of psychologists' overconcern with abnormal behavior, is a matter for particular regret because of the importance of psychological factors in pain. (One of the most influential of contemporary theories of pain was proposed jointly by a psychologist, R. Melzack, and a physiologist, P. Wall.)

Part of the explanation for psychologists' neglect of the subject can be traced to the fact that many of them share the widespread belief that pain experiences are determined solely by direct physical causes–burns, breaks, cuts, systemic dysfunctions, and so on. Psychological factors, it is conceded, are relevant but insignificant. This view reflects a conception of pain that is outdated.

Another reason for the neglect of pain research is the belief that pain, a secondary phenomenon, is of little interest in its own right. As Melzack points out in his valuable book, *The Puzzle of Pain*, "research time and money is devoted to many problems of obvious clinical significance, but pain, often considered the symptom and not the disease, receives far less attention" (p. 203).[1]

Our main aim in this chapter is to indicate some of the ways in which psychologists can contribute to an increased understanding of pain and how to modify it. The extent of the opportunities can be illustrated by two simple facts. Complaints of pain are an extremely common reason for seeking medical advice, and, as has been mentioned, psychological factors exert a major influence on pain experiences. The question is whether clinical psychologists as yet have anything practical to contribute.

The view that pain is always and necessarily a consequence (and indeed a symptom) of injury or physical illness is not entirely accurate. It is now evident that people without known organic pathology suffer pain, the validity of which cannot be doubted. Second, even when an organic basis for pain is established, psychological factors continue to affect the experience of pain (for instance, its quality, intensity, and duration). Then there are those extraordinary examples of people who experience little or no pain despite severe injuries. It is common knowledge that, during religious ceremonies but not at other times, dervishes are capable of enduring what would otherwise be extremely painful stimulation with apparent tranquillity. Anyone who has seen them pierce both cheeks with a sharp metal skewer, apparently painlessly, can never doubt the paramount importance of psychological factors.

Another striking example of the influence of such factors comes from a study reported by Beecher. He found that thirty-five out of 100 surgical patients experienced relief from pain after receiving a placebo when they were expecting morphine.[2] Their strong expectation that the pain would be reduced by the supposed injection of morphine was sufficient to bring relief.

The inadequacy of a conception of pain based on a direct one-to-one relationship between sensory input (for instance, tissue injury) and pain experience is obvious in cases of self-mutilation. Some psychologically disturbed patients, usually young women with personality disorders, deliberately and repeatedly injure themselves. The most common form of self-multilation is cutting of the face and arms. Characteristically, these patients report no pain when inflicting the injuries, even though these are often severe. Instead they describe feelings of relief and a decrease in tension. One of our patients, a seventeen-year-old girl, who repeatedly slashed her face (causing serious disfigurement), said that she experienced no pain from the injuries, although she was normally sensitive to pain incurred in other circumstances. Her explanation for this behavior was that feelings of unhappiness and a numb tension built up in her until they became intolerable, and she had learned that she could achieve rapid release from this tension by cutting herself. A period of relative calm then followed and she felt no pain from her wounds. In this, as in many other cases of self-injury, there was no relationship between the severity of the damage and the pain experience.

The concept of pain

Neglect of a psychological approach to the suffering of people in pain derives mainly from the long-established belief that the experience of pain is directly related to the amount of bodily damage or, exceptionally, to the intensity of stimulation. According to this view, the suffering results from and is proportional to the extent of the damage sustained; acceptance of this view leads to attempts to reduce the feedback of bodily damage to the central processing centers (for instance, by healing the damage or severing connecting fibers). Underlying these views is the specificity theory of pain proposed by von Frey, a German physiologist who worked at the universities of Leipzig and Würzburg at the turn of the century. In summary, he postulated the existence of specific pain receptors in body tissue that transmit distress messages directly to a pain center in the brain. He conceived of a relay system operating like a direct telephone link from the periphery to a central exchange, sometimes called the pushbutton theory. It is now agreed, however, that there are a number of pieces of clinical evidence that refute the direct-line relay model of the nervous system.[1] First, it has been shown that surgical interventions in the peripheral or central nervous system do not reliably produce permanent abolition of pain (e.g., cutting a peripheral nerve supply). According to the von Frey theory, if the distress messages are prevented from reaching the pain center, no pain should be felt. Thus studies in which surgical intervention has not reduced pain satisfactorily run contrary to specificity theory. Second, the theory cannot explain the occurrence of phantom limb pain, causalgia, and neuralgias. Phantom limb pain is a bizarre and distressing syndrome that occurs in approximately 35 percent of people who have had a limb amputated. The pain is usually felt as if it was located in the limb that has actually been lost – or the sufferer may report bizarre feelings, for example, that the fingers of his amputated hand are digging continuously into his palm. In about 5 percent of these cases the phantom pain persists in a severe form and may even worsen with time.

Livingstone reported a case of a physician who had had his arm amputated after being wounded by a pointed instrument (puncture wound).[3] "Not infrequently he had a sensation as if a sharp scalpel was being driven repeatedly, deep into the site of his original puncture wound. . . . In intervals between the sharper attacks of pain he experienced a persistent burning in the hand." Causalgias and neuralgias are pains that persist long after the occurrence of injuries to the peripheral nervous system and certainly long after the tissues have been repaired. Finally, pain is sometimes experienced in one part of the body after stimulation of an unrelated, nonpathological part of the body. (The interesting story of the development of von Frey's theory from three strands of evidence is well described and evaluated in Melzack's book.)

Not all of von Frey's assumptions have stood up to examination. One of the weakest parts of his theory is the assumption that the intensity of stimulation is in direct proportion to the perception of pain. The quality of the pain, its intensity, and its tolerability are influenced by a number of psychological variables that interact with the stimulation arising from the physical damage.

Before elaborating on these psychological determinants, we need to consider some valuable observations by Beecher.[2] He made the surprising claim that only about one-third of the severely wounded soldiers taken to a hospital from a battlefield requested pain killers; the majority either denied that they felt any pain or believed it to be too minor to require medication – despite their serious injuries. He notes that these soldiers were not suffering from shock and that they complained about injections as would any other patient. Beecher then compared the behavior of the combat group to that of a group of male civilian patients undergoing major surgery and thereby sustaining tissue injury, although of a less severe kind than that experienced by the soldiers. In the civilian group, four out of five patients requested medication to relieve their pain. He concluded that "the pain is in very large part determined by other factors, and of great importance here is the significance of the wound, i.e., reaction to the wound" (p. 165).

Beecher's observations and others of a similar character make plain some important weaknesses of specificity theory – the omission of psychological contributors to pain experience and the unsupported assumption of a direct relationship between tissue injury and pain. It is now evident that sensory stimulation, regarded as the single basis for pain in earlier theories, must take its place as the principal but not the sole factor in a complex experience. Among the psychological factors contributing to the experience are attitudes, beliefs, cultural views, moods such as anxiety and depression, focus of attention, motivation, and personality traits. We have now to deal with the many and interacting factors that cause pain and focus interest on the functional relationships between them. A pain over the heart may be intense and produce great suffering in someone unaware that it is probably due to indigestion. Another person, aware of the signs and significance of indigestion, is likely to regard the same pain as being weak and to be ignored. With the onset of the supposed "heart pain," the first sufferer will no longer notice a toothache that has been nagging at him. Simple examples of this type illustrate how one's attention to and interpretation of the significance of a pain can affect its quality and intensity.

A theory that has tried to come to grips with this more complex view of pain is that proposed by Melzack[1] and Wall – the *gate theory*, which postulates a mechanism that exercises selective control of stimulation. Without going into the intricacies of their position, it can be said that it appears to explain a number of findings regarding the recognition and coding of sensory information while strongly implicating psychological processes in the perception of pain. They have suggested that a strong influence is exerted by the brain on the transmission of information along the spinal cord. According to his hypothesis, pain "messages" coming from the periphery along the cord can be modified by messages moving downward from the brain. These downward influences include cognitive and other psychological states (such as attention, anxiety, and anticipation). The effects of such psychological variables are felt before the peripheral messages reach the brain. Although much more elaboration of how these influences operate is required, the inclusion of powerful downward influences is a useful expansion of the theory of pain. Many details of the thesis have come under criticism in the last few years,[4] and a number are reexamined in detail or restated by Wall.[5] Regardless of the outcome of the current debate, the gate control theory of pain has undoubtedly been "the most influential and important current theory of pain perception."[4] It not only explains a number of puzzling findings in pain perception and its clinical control, but has greatly influenced research. Pain perception and control can no longer be considered without acknowledging the importance of psychological variables.

Psychological factors

The factors of attention, suggestion, anxiety, and anticipation are known to have a significant effect on pain experiences; for instance, it is commonly observed that a minor injury sustained during some absorbing activity such as a game of football passes unnoticed. A standard injection given to a woman just as her baby is born (to aid detachment of the afterbirth) is seldom felt. Similar experiences can be reproduced in experiments in which the subject's attention is diverted during exposure to painful stimulation.

A complex set of psychological phenomena, which are usually summarized (rather unsatisfactorily) by the term "suggestion," certainly influence pain. Given the appropriate suggestion, hypnotized people report little or no pain from cuts and burns. Yogis in states of self-induced hypnosis or meditation readily carry out normally painful acts without evident pain. Reference has already been made to dervishes who put skewers through their cheeks. Some years ago one of us was able to observe an Indian religious ceremony in which devoted men, after a prolonged preparation of rhythmic chanting and dancing, walked along a path of glowing coals, without pain – or rather, without complaint of pain. Nor did they show overt signs of having undergone a painful experience.

In all these examples there is a strong element of suggestion operating, either self-suggestion or suggestion provided by others. In an experiment conducted to investigate the efficiency of intense auditory stimulation in reducing pain (audioanalgesia), Melzack and his colleagues obtained clear evidence of the role of suggestion in pain tolerance.[6] For experimental purposes they used artificially produced pain induced by the cold pressor test, in which the participants immerse their hands in an ice bath, which produces a deep, slow-rising pain. Three groups of people were used. One group recieved intense auditory stimulation as a pain reducer. The second group received the same auditory stimulation as well as a strong suggestion enhancing the value of this stimulation as a means of diminishing pain. The third group were told that ultrasonic sounds are powerful pain reducers, but then received only a low hum throughout the experimental period. The results showed that the participants who received intense auditory stimulation coupled with strong suggestion were able to keep their hands in the water significantly longer than those from either of the other two groups. The intense auditory stimulation alone did not raise pain tolerance; only when it was combined with the forceful influence of suggestion were satisfactory results achieved. A practical application of these and similar findings was made in the field of dentistry. Numbers of dentists, especially in the United States, installed earphones for their patients and allowed them to listen to music throughout their treatment. Unfortunately, the full significance of the accompanying suggestions were not widely known or accepted, and they were neglected by many of the dentists. Consequently, although many patients benefited from this form of pain reduction, considerable disappointment was also reported and, overall, the use of traditional analgesics in dentistry does not appear to have been greatly reduced.

Although it is premature to offer definitive statements, some evidence indicates that the procedure used in acupuncture for eliminating or reducing pain depends heavily on suggestions given by a firm believer in acupuncture to a suggestible patient. Based on Chinese traditional medicine, the procedure is capable of producing analgesia without the use of drugs. Needles are applied to particular parts of the body, and this results in a dulling or elimination of pain, either in the same part or in areas far from the location of the needles. The patient remains conscious throughout and is capable of conversing or even taking refreshment. According to Cheng and Ding,[7] it appears to work best on short operations and only on certain types of patients: "The success of the use of acupuncture analgesia depends on the willingness and understanding of the patients." They therefore select emotionally stable, intelligent individuals who are confident about the advantages of acupuncture. Melzack[8] has made an interesting attempt to explain some of the results within the gate control theory. He has shown a close relation between acupuncture points and traditional trigger areas. There can be few people, and certainly very few psychologists, who find no interest in this intriguing phenomenon.

Anxiety can have a considerable effect on both the quality and intensity of pain experiences. Patients who are anxious are more sensitive to pain and, as might be predicted from this, neurotic patients (who generally have high levels of anxiety) complain of pain more than others.[9] Leucotomy (a brain operation in which fibers joining the front section of the brain to the midbrain are severed), performed for the relief of pain, produces the best results in those patients whose anxiety is also markedly reduced by the operation. However, it appears that the operation alters rather than eliminates pain experiences. The pain is found to be less intrusive and less incapacitating, and in this sense can be said to be less distressing.

It has been estimated that 75 percent of postsurgical patients obtain marked relief from morphine. However, as we have seen, Beecher found that in many cases pain was greatly relieved after the administration of a placebo instead of the usual morphine.[2] Recalling Beecher's observation on wounded soldiers who needed far less treatment by analgesics than did hospital patients undergoing voluntary surgery, it seems certain that these two groups had different attitudes toward their injuries. The soldiers, after a period of stress in combat, found themselves alive and safe in a quiet ward. The voluntary patients, awakening in a ward and having varied expectations concerning the success of the operation and the associated pain and discomfort, would regard their surgical injuries very differently from battle wounds. The context and significance of the wound have a considerable effect on how much pain is suffered and reported. The concept of pain complaint, and its relation to pain experience, are interesting subjects but difficult to come to grips with simply because much of our information about pain experience is derived from pain complaints; hence it is difficult to disentangle the two. Pain experience and pain complaints are not necessarily synonymous. It is nevertheless interesting that the memory for pain can be surprisingly accurate – contrary to the common view that people are unable to recall pain qualities accurately.[10]

We need to bear in mind the cultural factors that enter into the style and frequency of complaining. For example, it is commonly observed that women make more pain complaints than men. This sex difference probably reflects the prevailing view of acceptable masculine behavior. Men are expected to complain less and endure more. Views and expectations of this sort also influence the behavior of doctors and nurses. For example, Bond and Pilowsky found that analgesics were often given by nurses in a way that was not consistent with the patients' own assessment of their pain or with their request for relief.[11] Women were given more powerful analgesics for less severe pain than were men, whose requests for relief were often ignored by the nursing staff. The influence of cultural factors is also seen in the variations of pain tolerance across different groups during similar experiences, such as childbirth. In his experiments, Hardy found a cultural variation; levels of radiant heat said by North Europeans to be merely warm evoked a different reaction from people of Mediterranean origin, who complained that they were painful.[12]

Valuable evidence on differences in pain tolerance was accumulated on a massive sample of 41,000 people tested at Stanford University. Woodrow and his colleagues found that men tolerate more pain than women, whites more than blacks, and blacks more than Asians. Pain tolerance decreased with age.[13]

Other psychological factors in pain experiences are the predictability of the pain and the possibility of exerting some control over it. In experimental work it has been shown that electric shocks are more bearable when the person can predict when or how strongly they will occur. The results of Janis (see Chapter 11), who found that patients had less postoperative pain when adequately informed and prepared, may be partly an outcome of this factor of predictability.[14] Some interesting experimental work in which variations in tolerance for pain were produced by preparing participants for painful experiences is consistent with this notion. "Rehearsals" of the anticipated pain have been found to increase tolerance, and the more similar the rehearsed experienced is to the pain to be experienced, the greater the increase in tolerance.

Personality differences have also been shown to affect complaining. Bond studied fifty-two women with carcinoma of the cervix to see how their personality traits and attitudes to the disease related to the pain they felt and their complaints.[15] He found that pain-free patients were less emotional and more sociable, whereas patients experiencing pain but not complaining of it were emotional but not sociable. Finally, the patients who were both emotional and sociable experienced and complained of considerable pain thereby receiving more medication. Bond suggests that personality characteristics of this type may help to explain the reluctance of some patients to consult their doctors, despite the onset of serious illness. It may also help to explain the varied success that different individuals have in obtaining treatment, including analgesics, from their doctors.

Personality differences are related to pain tolerance as well as complaint. Lynn and Eysenck used a thermostimulator technique, involving the application of steadily increasing degrees of heat, to assess pain tolerance in a group of students.[16] When they were divided on the basis of their personality scores, pain tolerance was found to increase with extraversion. On the other hand, introverts appeared to be more sensitive to painful stimulation. In related work, Sybil Eysenck investigated differences in pain experience during childbirth and concluded that personality differences affect not only the quality but also the intensity of the pain experienced.[17] As with the results obtained from students, she found that introverts, in contrast to extraverts, appeared to feel pain sooner and more intensely but to complain less, although they might remember the pain more vividly afterwards. Petrie has also contributed some interesting investigations in the field of individual differences.[18] She suggests that people can be grouped into two types on the basis of a test of kinaesthetic aftereffects in which the persisting effects of stimulation are assessed. "Augmenters" appear to overestimate sensory input whereas "reducers" diminish input. The results of these two groups on kinaesthetic tests correlated significantly with their personality scores and with differences in pain tolerance. She found that reducers had higher extraversion scores and greater tolerance of pain. Replication and development of her findings might well improve our understanding of the relationship and among personality, pain tolerance, and complaints of pain (see Eysenck's theory).[19]

In addition to anxiety, it seems likely that moods, such as depression or elation, the degree of alertness, and physical fatigue will prove to be important factors in pain experience.

Beecher was so convinced of the importance of psychological factors in determining what he called the "reaction component of pain" that he came to regard laboratory (and hence, artificial) investigations of pain as being virtually useless.[2] The significance of the injury, its importance in the person's life, his view of the situation in which the injury was sustained, the anxiety induced by the injury, and so on, cannot be adequately reproduced in the predictable conditions of a laboratory. He felt that these omissions would invalidate the research. Although his dismissal is too sweeping, some support for his view comes from the finding that analgesics that are completely reliable in clinical practice give variable results in experimentally induced pain. An important factor in the clinical effectiveness of these drugs is their psychological significance in the setting of hospital or doctor's office and the positive attitude of the doctor.

It is hard to escape the view that pain is a complex phenomenon dependent on sensory input and a number of psychological factors. The extent of the interaction between these two types of determinants has not been unravelled and is an inviting challenge for psychologists. Progress in clarifying these relationships would be a useful step toward a more practical approach in applying psychological expertise to the modification of pain.

Some of the most unbearable pains, such as cardiac pain, rise so rapidly in intensity that the patient is unable to achieve any control over them. On the other hand, some slowly rising temporal pains are suspectible to central control and may allow the person to think about something else or use other strategems to keep the pain under control [Melzack, p. 200].[1]

It seems evident that psychologists would do well to tackle these slowly rising pains frist.

General implications

What implications can be drawn from these observations of pain experience and behavior? First, we need to adopt a broader approach to the relief of pain. Many of the factors that affect experiencces of pain are either neglected or manipulated in ignorance by people who confine their attention to the physical determinants of pain–as conceived in von Frey's specificity theory. More than fifteen years ago Beecher felt that there was sufficient evidence already available "to lead future therapeutic research into the modification of the psychic reaction to the original sensation" (p. 189). Despite the fact that Beecher's views have been extensively quoted over the intervening years, the medical and ancillary professions, showing few signs of acknowledging the extraphysical components of pain, continue to treat it as if it were a simple and direct reflection of sensory disturbances. Patients still complain that many doctors do not seem prepared to take the time to allay their anxiety by providing explanations of their pain, or to give them details of impending painful events such as operations (see Chapter 11). Few systematic attempts have been made to employ specific psychological procedures to reduce pain. Instead we continue to rely almost exclusively on analgesic drugs and, in extreme cases, surgery.

Practical implications

As a step toward improvement in the psychological management of pain, we propose eight modification procedures that might be of some practical value.

1. Fully inform patients of expected discomforts from operations, deteriorating diseases, and so on. Give specific instructions concerning the type of pain that can be predicted to occur during the course of an illness, following an operation, in childbirth, and so on. Information should deal with the intensity of the pain, its location, quality, duration, likelihood of secondary discomforts (such as indigestion and urinary discomfort). If this were done, the patient would encounter few unexpected (and hence

potentially frightening), unpleasant sensations and by comprehending, almost certainly cope better with the symptoms and their side-effects.

2. Use desensitization (see Chapter 10) and specific anxiety-reduction techniques (already available in psychology) to deal with cases where the significance of the symptom or illness produces an unreasonable degree of fear.

3. Use suggestion as an aid in speeding recovery, reducing the intensity of pain, and so on.

4. As distraction can help in the attenuation of pain, assess the usefulness of developing a set of routines for patients that would enable them to turn their concern and attention away from the symptom or painful part.

5. Teach self-control procedures (see Chapter 8) for the reduction of specific symptoms (such as specific muscular relaxation for secondary symptoms such as headache).

6. Design instructions to improve the detection by the patient of his or her need for further medication, thereby increasing self-control and prediction.

7. Give social attention and other rewards contingent on the reduction of complaints of pain -especially relevant in cases of chronic pain problems. Promptly give praise and attention for statements and actions indicating improvements.

8. In cases of self-mutilation, turn all these methods upside-down if necessary. If we reformulate the problem raised by these patients, we can think of a new aim for treatment–by regarding the problem as one of *lowering* their pain thresholds, we might then consider ways of elevating their anxiety, focusing full attention on the wound, rewarding them by increased attention when they make pain complaints, and so on. Obviously these possibilities will need to be explored with great care.

Having entered the field so late, psychologists are faced with a host of tasks and problems, and many of them will need to specialize in the study of pain. Melzack goes so far as to recommend the establishment of special clinics for the study and treatment of pain:

The pain clinic would allow the development of a battery of techniques to control pain. The pharmacological, sensory, and psychological methods of pain control do not exclude each other. A combination of several methods–such as electrical stimulation of nerves and appropriate drugs–may be necessary to provide satisfactory relief. The effective combination may differ for each type of pain and possibly for each individual depending on such factors as the patient's earlier medical history, pattern of spread of trigger zones, and the duration of pain; but it is only in a clinic, where many cases are seen and complete data files are kept, that sufficient experience and knowledge can be acquired to allow the best judgement in each case [p. 202].[1]

Future directions

We can summarize some of the tasks of psychologists:

1. The manipulation of psychological variables to produce an effect on present pain experience or to prepare an individual for predicted painful events. The physical recovery itself may also prove to be affected by psychological factors of the types discussed.

2. Development of more sophisticated methods for assessing subjective pain experiences, pain behavior and complaints.

3. Investigation of pain from four points of view: pain thresholds, subjective experiences, pain complaints, and pain behavior (seeking help, self-medication, etc.) A case history reported by Fordyce and his colleagues provides an interesting example of interdependence.[20] They described the treatment of a man who had complained of pain for many years, by changing the social consequences of his complaints of pain. Successful treatment of the complaint behavior was followed by a marked decrease in pain behavior (which had included withdrawal from daily activities, persistent resting, and so on). Unfortunately, they did not report his subjective estimates of the intensity of the pain, but one can infer that they must have decreased as the patient was able to return to normal activities after being incapacitated for eighteen years. When progress has been made along these lines, it should be possible to gauge the effect of psychological factors on each aspect of the pain phenomena. It is also likely that a high rate of complaining sustains and even increases pain. There is almost certainly a high correlation between pain complaint and pain behavior. It follows that reductions of any one of these four aspects of pain may lead to some reduction in the others. Naturally the interdependence and independence of these four components are matters of great interest for researchers and, we predict, will occupy the attention of psychologists for some considerable time.

4. Research into specific treatment techniques, which might include the development of distraction routines, relaxation methods, testing the efficacy of suggestions, specific procedures to reduce anxiety about the outcome of an illness or operation, and so on. The biofeedback method (see Chapter 8) is a promising development which may help people to gain control of a specific biological subsystem. Its application in the treatment of certain types of headache is discussed in the next chapter.

5. Research into the relation between personality variables and the four major components of pain – thresholds, subjective experience, complaints, and overt behavior – offers intriguing possibilities.

5   A psychological approach to headaches

In the previous chapter a case was made for the introduction of psychological expertise into the study of pain. Headaches are a practical and common example to choose. The study of headaches is noteworthy for a profusion of psychological terms and concepts and for the absence of psychologists. It is to be hoped that the imminent arrival of psychologists will lead to the disappearance of the psychological claptrap that currently passes for explanation.

A valuable study of the prevalence of headaches in the community was carried out by Waters in a circumscribed area on a random selection of people selected from voter registration lists.[1] Sixty-five percent of the men and 79 percent of the women in the sample reported that they had suffered from headaches in the previous year. In other surveys even higher figures were obtained.[2] Although it is not possible to establish exactly how costly headaches are in terms of suffering, money spent on medication, or working time lost, the figures are certain to be large. Some of the difficulties in obtaining precise estimates are the high rate of self-medication and the fact that headaches are seldom regarded as being sufficiently serious to require extended time off work. Hence formal medical reports do not reflect the true incidence of headaches. However, it is possible to obtain some rough estimates of the extent of the problem by examining the approximate expenditure on headaches. In the United States in 1976, total consultation costs for headache and migraine were estimated at $110 million, and prescription costs were approximately $33.5 million. In Britain (1977–78) a total of £13.3 million were spent on headache consultations and prescribed medication.[3] Despite the approximate nature of these estimates, they indicate the size of the problem. In yet another survey confined to a preselected two-day period, nearly 50 percent of the respondents in two American cities reported that they had taken self-prescribed pain-relievers during the 48-hour period under study,[4] and we know from other sources that the greatest proportion of self-prescribed pain-relievers are taken in order to subdue head pains. So in terms of prevalence alone, headaches are a significant clinical problem for psychologists who hope to increase our understanding of pain problems and, in time, to contribute psychological techniques for modifying pain. If psychologists need other inducements to concern themselves with the problems of headache, perhaps they will be provoked into action by the uncritical use of psychological concepts prevalent in the literature. For example, in a well-known text, muscular-contraction headaches are attributed to "psychosexual conflicts" and "unresolved dependency needs."[5] It is not merely that assertions of this kind are made in the absence of supporting evidence; there seems to be general agreement that psychological evidence is superfluous.

Less than half of the identified sufferers from headaches consult a medical practitioner for this complaint. What happens to those people who do seek treatment from a doctor? At present headaches are dealt with predominantly by general practitioners and neurologists. In daily practice numbers of them appear to rely on a conception of pain that we have argued is now outdated. In both diagnosis and management, sensory input is held to be the most important factor, be it arterial constriction/dilation or muscular contraction, or both. Attempts at diagnosis and pharmacological intervention are directed toward detection and reduction of this type of input to a central processing mechanism. In the case of detection doctors try to establish the presence of physical changes by examining the symptoms (nausea, tenderness of the back of the neck and shoulders, etc.) produced by the postulated dysfunction or injury; in the case of reduction, the purpose is to restore the muscle or artery to normal functioning.

It would be wrong to assume, however, that there is no concern for psychological factors. Virtually all writers stress (probably incorrectly) that certain personality traits and attitudes are characteristic of headache sufferers. A special committee of neurologists and other physicians, convened in the United States in 1962 in an attempt to clarify the definitions of different types of headaches, concluded that both physical and psychological factors contribute to the production of headaches. Indeed, both factors were included in the formal definitions of headache.[6]

Many writers also emphasize the importance of psychological factors in the long-term amelioration of headaches. For example, Friedman, in his discussion of migraine, states that "in the ability of the patient to handle emotional tension lies the most satisfactory means of preventing the attacks in the majority of cases" (p. 777). In his discussion of muscular-contraction headaches, he invokes "mental conflicts" as a key factor and recommends psychotherapy to relieve emotional tension and stress. In similar style, the author of a standard text on headaches says that the successful management of this problem requires no less than the "amelioration and elimination of dissatisfaction and discontent" (p. 616).[8]

In most of the literature, there is an imbalance between the assumptions on which diagnosis and treatment are based (especially the idea of blocking or reducing the input from the area of damage to the pain center) and the acknowledged relevance of psychological factors to both etiology and treatment. The significance of psychological factors is often noted but seldom acted upon. In consequence, practitioners are left with little choice but to offer fatuous advice of the character quoted above. It can be argued, however, that this gap in health care reflects more unfavorably on psychologists than on the medical profession.

Diagnosis and treatment

Before considering the contribution that psychologists can make, it is advisable briefly to review the prevailing practices and ideas on the subject. Ninety percent of chronic sufferers from headache experience either muscular-contraction headaches, vascular headaches of the migraine type, or a combination of the two.[8] Of the total population of headache sufferers, only a tiny percentage suffer from injury or disease. In these cases, the headache is associated with or results from cranial trauma, hypertension, tumor, and so on. In an epidemiological study carried out by Waters, the prevalence of classical migraine was estimated to be 4 percent in men and 7 percent in women.[9] Data from other surveys indicate that muscle-contraction headaches are three to four times more common than the migraine type. As we shall see, however, there are some difficulties in distinguishing satisfactorily between migraine and other types of headache.

Although many people refer to any recurrent severe headache as migraine, this loose usage is unhelpful. The special committee on headaches, referred to earlier, differentiated no less than fifteen different categories of headache.[6] However, for our purposes we can confine ourselves to the three most common of them. In classical migraine, it is said the onset of the headache is unilateral, preceded by visual prodromata (warnings) and is accompanied by feelings of nausea and sometimes vomiting. It is said to be associated with a family history of similar headache, although Waters failed to confirm this. The quality of the pain is often described as "throbbing" as opposed to "aching."[5] It is also stressed that migraine often occurs during periods of relaxation, a feature that is said to distinguish it from the headaches attributed to muscle tension. It is widely believed that migraine results from vasoconstriction (narrowing of blood vessels) of certain intercranial arteries, followed by vasodilation (widening of the vessels) and distension, especially affecting the external carotid, the principal artery in the neck. Despite this view, for practical purposes, diagnosis is generally based on the patient's subjective reports of symptoms. Objective demonstration of vaso-constriction or dilation of vessels is rarely required, and these changes have been monitored in surprisingly few studies. Different clinicians and writers on the subject tend to base their diagnosis on varying sets of the symptoms mentioned, and to give them different degrees of importance. At present the three basic symptoms that appear to satisfy most authorities are unilaterality, sensory prodromata, and nausea or vomiting. But when any one of these three is lacking and other factors are present, it is left to the diagnostician to make a judgment as to how the headache is to be classified. Presumably many of the doubtful cases could be clarified if greater use was made of physiological measurements of constriction, dilation, and so on.

The second major type is muscular-contraction headache or, as it was previously called, "psychogenic" headache. The diagnosis of this type of headache is not entirely satisfactory despite the apparent simplicity of the definition offered by the special committee. "Ache or sensation of tightness or pressure, or constriction, widely varied in intensity, frequency and duration... commonly suboccipital. It is associated with sustained contraction of skeletal muscles in the absence of permanent structural change"[6]

No measurement of the muscle tension associated with the locus of the symptom (on the head, neck, or shoulders) is required for the diagnosis, although this is included as a diagnostic feature in the definition quoted. There is research evidence, however, that in these cases muscle tension is in fact increased between and during headaches.[9–10] However, our own research leads us to conclude that the connection between muscle tension and this type of headache is not always as direct or obvious as is generally supposed. We found that migraine sufferers had significantly higher tension in the frontalis muscle than the so-called muscle-tension headache sufferers.[11–12] Although muscle-tension headache patients did show significantly more frontalis muscle tension than people who do not suffer from headaches, it is clear that the presence of elevated muscle tension cannot be used as a basis for making a diagnostic distinction between migraine and tension headaches. In addition, we found that the correlations among muscle-tension level, headache intensity and frequency, and pain behavior were surprisingly low. Epstein[13] and his colleagues confirm the low correspondence of frontalis muscle activity and self-report of pain in muscular-contraction sufferers. They report a lack of association between muscle activity and self-report estimates, except in certain individuals. Clearly the relation between muscle-tension levels and the occurrence of a tension headache is more complex than was formerly thought to be the case. It is necessary to determine what variables, other than electromyographic (EMG) levels, influence pain reports.

In practice, muscle-tension headaches tend to be identified by a process of exclusion. That is, they are headaches that neither result from organic disease, nor are associated with migraine symptoms. They are headaches with bilateral onset, absence of nausea, no prodromata, and little or no throbbing.

One of the major problems in attempting to arrive at discrete diagnoses is that many factors are common to the two types of headache. This is not altogether surprising, as it is more than likely that a severe attack of migraine may produce secondary muscular contractions as a response to the pain. Similarly, severe attacks of muscle-contraction headache may result in secondary vasoconstriction of the relevant arteries. These mixed types of headache, comprising a combination of muscular and vascular symptoms, form the third major group. The sharp distinction drawn between vascular and muscular headaches appears to be convenient, if not precise. It is possible that there is a continuum from mild to severe headaches, and that the effect of vascular changes becomes greater in association with severity. Support for this hypothesis comes from the investigation of EMG levels, in which four separate researchers have reported migraine cases to have higher muscle tension than so-called tension cases.[12] It is to be hoped that psychologists will in time make a contribution to clarifying the similarities and distinctions between these different types of headaches.

There are many beliefs concerning the personality of headache sufferers that tend to be perpetuated by writers who depend almost entirely on clinical impression. The traditional beliefs about sufferers are that they are more intelligent, more neurotic, overcontrolled, and so on. Claims about their distinctive personality are well illustrated in the following quotation from Friedman, which is characteristic of others.[5-14] Friedman writes that "[the migraine sufferer shows] adult perfectionism, rigidity, resentment, ambitiousness, efficiency, a constitutional predisposition to sustained emotional states" (p. 774).[7] And again a few pages later, he writes of their "inflexibility, overconscientiousness, meticulousness, perfectionism, and resentment" (p. 776). Martin and his colleagues summarized their view of the personality problems of muscle-contraction headaches cases in this way: "Poorly repressed hostility is often evident, but unresolved dependency needs and psychosexual conflicts are also frequently present" (p. 203).[15] Even though these character sketches or "vignettes" are not supported by studies with control groups of matched age, sex, and so on, the beliefs continue to be perpetuated, particularly by doctors using a psychoanalytic framework.

It is also believed that migraine sufferers are not only more intelligent and predominantly from the professional classes, but that they have more visual defects, higher blood pressure, and a strong family history of migraine. None of these claims was substantiated in the systematic investigations reported by Waters.[1-9] He studied the association between the three main headache groups and the following characteristics: intelligence, social class, visual defects, level of blood pressure, and family prevalence. When the results were compared with those obtained from appropriate control cases, none of the hypotheses was confirmed.

Few writers offer a description of sufferers from muscular-contraction headaches that is distinctly different; the demoralizing lists of problems attributed to them rarely differ in length or in content from those used in describing migraine headaches. Despite the claims for the existence of clear diagnostic categories, the fact that the personality descriptions of tension-headache sufferers rarely differ from those ascribed to migraine cases reflects the uncritical reliance placed by nonpsychological workers on psychoanalytic writings, from which no differential explanations about headache can be derived. Certainly very few psychologists would have the courage to launch into generalizations about personality in the manner quoted here-for example, "migraine sufferers are more rigid, ambitious, resentful,"[16] and so on. These lists of labels are rarely worth serious consideration. If all the personality labels applied to headache patients were substantiated, they would be indistinguishable from a disturbed psychiatric population. When the necessary research is eventually carried out, few of the traditional beliefs about the relationship between personality and headache are likely to survive. Certainly, the early indications reinforce our suspicions about the falsity of most of these traditional ideas about the personality of headache sufferers. In a random sample of headache sufferers drawn from a general practice in London, it was found that the patients did not differ in any significant respect from the members of the general population on four important dimensions of personality.[17] Their scores on neurotic tendency, extraversion, psychoticism, and on dissimulation, as measured on the personality questionnaire developed by Eysenck and Eysenck,[18] fell within the appropriate range for a normal sample. Moreover, there were no personality differences between migraine sufferers, muscle-contraction headache sufferers, and mixed cases. We did, however, come across one piece of information that may help to explain the origin of some traditional beliefs about headache sufferers. The subgroup of sufferers who had taken their complaints to a specialist neurologist returned scores indicating a significantly higher degree of neurotic tendency. One wonders if the prevailing medical views of the personality of headache sufferers might not have been molded by the fact that the people who seek specialized help for their complaint are uncharacteristically neurotic.

It is also worth remembering that many of the difficulties reported by headache sufferers, apart from the pain and discomfort, may as easily be understood as a response to the experience of chronic pain and the consequent disruption of their lives and responsibilities.[19] A priori, one can predict that a chronic complaint such as migraine will lead to resentment, irritability, and even depression. A prominent physiologist, Rodbard,[20] has given this description: "Like other discomforts, the sensation of severe pain impresses itself so vividly upon the attention of the patient that his search for relief becomes a primary activity . . . he may exhibit progressive irritability and aversive behavior . . . and he will finally project strong feelings against persons or objects in his environment. Relief of the discomfort eliminates the emotional disturbance within a few seconds" (p. 184).

Most types of treatment are pharmacological, especially in cases of classical migraine. But in the light of current views on the role of psychological factors in the cause of migraines, it is usually thought desirable to provide psychotherapy to help the sufferer cope with emotional conflicts. This recommendation is especially evident in discussions of the treatment for tension headaches. Despite these views on the need for psychotherapy, we have not located any studies in which the efficacy of psychotherapy for headache cases has been assessed. The shortage of evidence may be attributed in part to the fact that the recommended course of psychotherapy is rarely offered or accepted.

Some interesting results on the efficacy of pharmacological treatments have been reported. In several studies, the most commonly recommended treatment for migraine, ergotamine, was found to be more effective than a placebo,[21] but in others no difference was detected.[1] A comparative evaluation of the effects of ergotamine is hampered by the fact that different therapists administer the substance in varying ways. Drug prophylaxis has not been shown to be superior to the placebo effect.[22] Muscular relaxants, tranquilizers, analgesics, and antidepressants are all used in the treatment of tension headaches, but control trials are hard to come by. However, it is commonly said that there are large individual differences in response to these drugs. An interesting point was made in a case report by Friedman, who noted that although the prescribed drugs reduced muscle tension, his patient continued to complain of tension headaches.[23] This finding can only increase doubts about the central role ascribed to muscle contractions in "muscular-contraction headache," a defintion that unfortunately incorporates a cause. It is commonly held that a substantial proportion of the headache population suffers from underlying depression and that antidepressants should be prescribed.[16-24] It remains unclear how justified the depression diagnosis is, and if the antidepressant drugs are effective.[22] Headaches are more common in a psychiatric population than in a general practice sample, but they occur predominantly in anxiety neurotic, neurotic depression, and personality disorder groups rather than in the psychiatric depression groups.[25] However, the results are difficult to interpret because of diagnostic confusions and sampling inadequacies.

The use of drugs to produce muscular relaxation presupposes a high, if not perfect, correlation between muscle-tension level and pain-intensity frequency and the associated behavior (i.e., frequency of medication). This supposition is undermined by recent evidence of the low correspondence between the level of muscle tension and the appearance of the features of pain referred to.[11] A recent case illustrates this point. A young woman complained that she was suffering from moderately intense headaches every day. Although her medication frequency and intensity of complaint were both very high, psychophysiological recordings revealed no abnormality of muscle tension or muscle reactivity. In the absence of these physiological findings, it might have been concluded (incorrectly) from her complaints that she would benefit from taking muscular relaxants. In this case, the sharp discordance between complaint level and pain behavior, and muscle state, merited psychological investigation.

Psychological research possibilities

The fact that psychologists have contributed little to the treatment of headaches is the clearest possible indication of the need for a period of research. Restricting ourselves mainly to those issues discussed in our brief review of the present state of headache control, we shall try to sketch some of the opportunities for psychologists that are now beginning to emerge.

Although the mechanisms that precipitate the two main types of headache (migraine and tension headache) are generally agreed to be vascular and muscular, respectively, objective measurements of these two types of function are rarely made when reaching diagnostic decisions. Psychophysiologists, with their specialized training in the recording and analysis of bodily functions of these types, have much to offer. In

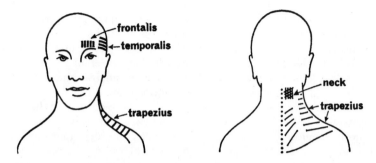

Figure 2 Head and neck muscles.

the case of tension headaches, they could record contractions of the muscle in the head and neck (trapezius, neck frontalis, temporalis, etc., see Figure 2) during headache and headache-free episodes. Our preliminary finds have revealed a surprising degree of specificity of muscle tension; not all four of these muscles are necessarily implicated in the occurrence of headaches in any particular patient.[11]

Although they present some technical problems, recordings can also be made of the vasoconstriction and dilation of extracranial temporal arteries. Recordings of this character would enable psychologists to collaborate in the investigation of such problems as the following. (1) Can the hypothesized distinction among vascular, muscular, and mixed headaches can be confirmed by objective measurements? Recordings carried out on mixed cases might also help to clarify which type of pharmacological (or other) treatment is most appropriate (for instance, a muscle relaxant). (2) By measuring the changes in key arteries and muscles between and during headaches, can we learn whether there are signs of a return to normal between attacks or whether basal levels are persistently elevated? If the resting levels are found to be high (and there is some evidence that this is so),[26] this might explain why in many cases headaches are said to occur after relatively minor stimulation.

Careful psychophysiological research will also help to clarify the putative role of the frontalis muscle in tension headaches. This muscle, the most common locus of pain in this type of headache, may be a particularly difficult one to relax. Even when the patient is able generally to relax his or her body, it is not uncommon to find that the frontalis muscle is still partly contracted. For example, Balshan investigated the activity of sixteen different muscle groups and found that all but two of them showed highly correlated activity.[27] The exceptions were the frontalis and sternomastoid muscles. The resting level of tension in the frontalis muscle was found to be far above that of the other fifteen muscles, both during rest and stimulation. This poor relationship between a generally relaxed state of the muscles and the continuing tension of the frontalis needs clarification. However, there is some confusion concerning the amount of activity in the frontalis. Some researchers have found little tension in this muscle.[12] Further work is needed to clarify this issue, and procedures for relaxing this muscle, where necessary, are needed.

For the most part, doctors assess the quality of pain experiences on a rough subjective scale. This may consist of a five- or seven-point scale, ranging from "no headache" to "mild headache," right up to "incapacitatingly severe" headache. Although this sort of rough estimate has its uses, most obviously in daily practice, something more refined is needed when carrying out research into the quality of pain experiences. A new questionnaire developed by Melzack and Torgenson to assess twenty different qualities of pain experience, each along a dimension of intensity, may facilitate further investigations of this type of question.[28] The respondent has to indicate which adjectives, in a list provided, best describe the pain – for example, flickering, beating, quivering, throbbing, pounding, pulsing, and so on. We can illustrate the possibilities of this type of approach with an example. Although there is a strong belief that vascular headaches are "throbbing" whereas muscular ones are "aching," no adequate study has been performed in which the intensity of the pain experienced is used as a covariant. In other words, it may be that as a headache increases in intensity, it is more likely to be described as "throbbing." Our own research indicates that intense headaches are significantly more likely to be vascular in origin than muscular.[29] Research using a scale of the type developed by Melzack, with separate dimensions for quality and intensity, permits analysis of the type of question.

Although psychologsts' contributions to treatment have so far been confined to explorations with the techniques of relaxation and of biofeedback (see Chapter 8), they are in a strong position to contribute methodologically to the design of controlled trials to assess the efficacy of psychotherapeutic and pharmacological treatment. In seeking a comprehensive view of treatment effects, it might be desirable to measure physiological changes (e.g., frontalis tension), pain complaints (quality and intensity as well as duration and frequency), and pain behavior itself. If research on the not dissimilar subject of fear is any guide,[30] it will be found that although these three variables are well correlated, they show a degree of independent variation. It is likely that a certain amount of desynchrony will be encountered, with the three measures changing at different speeds. Our own research has shown that when one succeeds in lowering muscle tension by biofeedback, desynchronous adjustments of pain intensity and pain behavior can be observed. As is the case with the modification of fear, the three measures resumed a synchronous relationship during the follow-up period.[31]

Awareness of the occurrence of desynchronous changes is of practical as well as theoretical interest, in that therapeutic conclusions drawn from the changes observed in one of the three variables may give a misleading picture. The possibility of desynchrony relates to a suggestion made in the previous chapter, that psychological factors may play a more significant role in less severe pain. Consequently, as intense pains diminish, the deliberate manipulation of attention, suggestion, and other psychological factors should expedite further improvements. Once one has determined the level at which psychological factors can be successfully manipulated, it becomes possible to reduce drug dosages and finally withdraw them.

There are several strategies that psychologists might employ in their approach to the problems of pain control. In the first place, they could attempt to reduce pain levels and complaint by means of relaxation training. The extent to which these procedures affect resting levels of muscle tension, as opposed to calming the mental state, is as yet unclear. A second possibility is the development of various techniques for coping with trigger stimuli that are known to precipitate headaches. For example, social anxiety and neurotic fears are said to produce headaches when people with these types of vulnerability are placed in social situations. If this is confirmed, treatment techniques such as desensitization or flooding (see Chapter 10) should prove to be therapeutically useful. A fourth approach is one that deals with the extent to which pain complaints are sustained by the reaction of others. Research on other types of complaint behavior has shown that the frequency of this behavior is determined in part by the manner in which other people respond to it. Intense and regular interest shown in the sufferers' complaints will probably increase the frequency of complaining, whereas comparative indifference is likely to be followed by a decline in the frequency of complaining. Modification of the patient's expectation of the attention that follows excessive complaining entails giving advice not only to the patient but also to the people who have a major part in the patient's life. It was observed in the case study mentioned on page 41[32] that disregard for the headache complaints of a chronic sufferer, combined with increased attention and social rewards for healthy activities unrelated to the sufferer's preoccupation with headaches, greatly reduced the amount of the complaints. Although it is easy to elaborate further plans for psychological research in headaches, we have no desire to compose lists of unrealistic schemes. Our principal aim is to show how psychologists and physicians can combine their interests and expertise in opening new avenues.[33]

6 Sleep disorders

Disorders of sleep are extremely common. The most frequent complaints are of insomnia – difficulty in falling asleep or in staying asleep. It has been estimated in surveys that from one-sixth to one-quarter of the adult population is affected by sleep problems,[1-3] and in psychiatric conditions this proportion rises to 45 percent. In addition to insomnia, there are sleep disorders that affect only a small number of people. These include such problems as somnambulism (sleep walking), head banging, nocturnal bed wetting (enuresis), night terrors, and nightmares.

Intense research over the past two decades has increased our knowledge about sleep, but may problems remain. We are still unclear about the function of sleep and how much of it we need in order to feel refreshed, satisfied, and capable of normal functioning. Expansion of physiological knowledge has outstripped psychological understanding, and this uneven development helps to account for the narrowness of prevailing approaches to treatment.

As doctors generally prescribe sleeping pills (hypnotics) for insomnia, there is a large consumption of these drugs. In 1974, approximately 6 percent of the drug prescriptions in England and Wales were for hypnotics[4] (barbiturate and nonbarbiturate). Although there has been a trend toward reduced prescription and sales of barbiturates in both the United Kingdom and the United States, hypnotic nonbarbiturate prescriptions have nearly quadrupled in Britain (1964–74),[5] and their sales in the United States between 1973 and 1977 increased from approximately $30 million to $50 million.[4]

Dunlop has estimated that in Britain one night's sleep in ten is induced by hypnotic drugs.[6] Or, to put it another way, using his estimate as a basis, we can say that on any night 3.5 million people in England and Wales will take sleeping pills. Despite its evident popularity, we hope to show why an exclusively pharmacological approach to treatment is not satisfactory.

As we have said, research into sleep has been predominantly physiological and pharmacological, with a sprinkling of psychological studies. Regrettably little work has been carried out on the psychological question of central importance – sleep satisfaction. It is undoubtedly as important to know how much sleep is required for psychological as for physical restoration. At present we have little reason for supposing that the two types of needs, physical and psychological, are always fulfilled simultaneously. Nor do we know whether both needs are met by the same amount or the same type of sleep. It seems likely that individual differences in psychological need will be greater than the differences in physical need, given comparable physical exertions, stature, and so on. As many people who complain of sleeplessness do not in fact sleep for shorter periods than do good sleepers, it is important to determine the factors that affect a person's judgment of how long, and how well, he or she sleeps. Considerations of this type lead naturally to questions of how psychologists can best contribute to the understanding and modification of sleep disorders. But before examining the possibilities, it is necessary to give a short account of the nature of sleep.

The nature of sleep

A strong daily pattern of sleeping and waking develops with age. Babies gradually adopt a pattern of sleeping at night and being awake during the day; at 1 year old they have two phases of sleep (night and afternoon nap), and by 5 years old they usually follow the pattern of their parents. Babies average about 16.6 hours of sleep a day, but as they grow and mature children require less sleep. By the age of 30 to 40 most people average about 7.4 hours of sleep each day, and this amount declines slowly until, at the age of 70, one may sleep as little as 6 hours in 24. Taking the adult population as a whole, the average nightly sleep is roughly 7.5 hours. It is important to remember, however, that there are large individual differences at all ages but particularly in the very young and the very old. There is also a small number of adults who appear to be adequately refreshed after as little as 3 or 4 hours of sleep. For most people this small ration would amount to insomnia, but for the lucky small percentage it appears to produce no problems and has been called "healthy insomnia."[7]

Contrary to earlier beliefs, sleep is not a period of mental and physical inactivity. It is an active process during which incessant but so far poorly understood mental activity continues, though in a different form from that which occurs during waking hours. Originally, the depth of sleep was estimated by ascertaining the amount of external stimulation necessary to awaken a sleeper. However, in recent years this has been supplemented, and almost replaced, by measures of the electrical activity of the brain (EEG), popularly known as brain waves.

When a person is awake and alert but with his or her eyes closed, brain waves of eight to thirteen cycles per second (the alpha rhythm) can be recorded from the back of the head.[8] With the onset of drowsiness these alpha rhythms gradually decrease, and the person reports a drifting or floating of consciousness. The onset of sleep is commonly defined as the point at which these rhythms disappear; consciousness is lost and responses to external stimuli are greatly diminished. Sleep can be divided into two major classes: rapid eye movement sleep (REM or paradoxical) and non-rapid eye movement sleep (non-REM or orthodox sleep). REM sleep, as the name suggests, is characterized by frequent bursts of rapid jerky eye movements and these are accompanied by very slow brain waves (two to six cycles per second) of a low voltage. In non-REM sleep there are very few rapid eye movements, and although the brain waves continue at a slow rate, they are of high voltage and faster frequency (twelve to fourteen cycles per second). Most research workers subdivide non-REM sleep into a further four stages on the basis of small differences in brain-wave patterns, but for our purposes these details of sleep stages are not pertinent. Further information is available in the texts by Kleitman[9] and Oswald.[8]

In the early stages of research into this new classification of sleep, dreaming was believed to occur only when the eyes moved rapidly (REM sleep). It is certainly true that about 75 percent of people awakened from REM sleep have been dreaming, in contrast to only about 7 percent of those in orthodox sleep. However, it now seems probable that REM periods are more associated with dreaming in the sense of fantasy occurrences, where as non-REM periods are associated with "thinking" of recent events or experiences. Although we can recall precious little of it, it appears that we dream for at least two out of the average seven-and-a-half hours we sleep each night. During the rest of the sleep period we probably "think" a great deal.

Sleep deprivation

Experience of depriving people of all or part of their sleep has revealed how essential sleep is for normal functioning; it has also shown the relative importance of certain types or stages of sleep. It is sometimes claimed that after prolonged deprivation of sleep, people become acutely disturbed and exhibit bizarre behavior. Certainly some extraordinary cases have been reported, but the appearance of extremely disturbed behavior depends on many factors including the individual's mental stability, physical condition, and expectations. On the whole it is true that unstable or disturbed people are more susceptible to the adverse effects of sleep deprivation. For most people the behavioral changes seen after deprivation are predictable and in addition to fatigue include irritability, inability to concentrate, and periods of disorientation and misperception. Lapses occur in the performance of tasks, particularly when the person is required to respond quickly. Although complete restoration of function takes a few days, we are fortunate in having the capacity for quick recovery. Even after going without sleep for as long as 200 hours, remarkable reversals can occur after a single long sleep (twelve to fourteen hours). Williams found a 90 percent recovery of efficiency after one such sleep,[10] but in his particularly careful research Wilkinson detected the persistence of subtle difficulties.[11]

During "recovery sleep" a rebound phenomenon is consistently observed. It appears that after deprivation there is a need for certain types of sleep. This is inferred from the fact that the percentage of time spent in particular stages of sleep shows a marked increment for a period before it returns to the sleeper's usual level. The rebound effect is strongest after loss of REM sleep, which is the first to be "repaid" after a period of total sleep deprivation. If, instead of total restriction of sleep, one merely prevents one type of sleep, the same rebound phenomenon is seen to occur even within the period of sleep itself.

Sleeping pills

The effects of sleep-inducing drugs have been fully investigated by EEG analyses. The sleep patterns of drug users have been documented and the effects of drug withdrawal of their brain-wave patterns have also been studied. Because of the widespread prescription of hypnotic drugs to people complaining of sleep difficulties, it is worth reviewing the main findings. Kales notes that "most physicians are unfamiliar with the basic sleep and dream cycles and the changes induced in them by hyponotic agents. Therefore they do not often ask patients how they sleep after sleeping pills have been prescribed or withdrawn."[12] In fact, virtually all the hyponotics produce similar disturbances of sleep pattern. Characteristically, there is a suppression of REM activity and of sleep stages III and IV, coupled with a marked delay in the occurrence of the first REM period. Upon withdrawal of the drug, especially after chronic use, there is a rebound effect in which the first REM time increases. Disturbances can also occur during this period and include nightmares, insomnia, and dissatisfaction with the quality of sleep. Most hyponotic drugs provide only brief therapeutic gain for larger losses: the disturbance of sleep rhythms, addiction, and withdrawal symptoms.[13] Unfortunately, psychologists have so far shown little interest in the question of *psychological restoration* following the use of hypnotic drugs. It is true that after taking these drugs the person will probably fall asleep more quickly and sleep for a longer period. However, as there will be insufficient REM sleep, there may be adverse psychological consequences of this deprivation despite the fact that the person is sleeping through the night.

A large proportion of people suffering from insomnia have psychiatric disorders–depression, anxiety neuroses, and so on. As many of these patients already experience less REM sleep (they do not merely sleep for a shorter time), treatment with hyponotic drugs may inadvertently aggravate some aspects of their sleep problems. It is possible that some of the symptoms are exacerbated by a loss of REM sleep. As Hawkins put it, "Hypnotic drugs do not have any substantive value for chronic insomnia and may in fact compound the problem due to the additional disruptions in pattern.[14] The rebound effects experienced after withdrawal of sleeping pills may contribute to the development of a dependence on these drugs, particularly if the doctor fails to prepare the patient for after-effects, the most notable of which are nightmares. Gradual withdrawal, with supportive explanations of the expected drug-induced physiological alterations in sleep pattern and their psychological consequences, may well be of importance. A careful psychological study of the role of doctors in preventing dependence on sleeping pills is overdue.

We need a psychology of sleep to complement the physiology of sleep. In particular, we require far more psychological information about the subjective reports that people give of their sleep experiences and satisfactions (and how to relate these to psychological assessments of sleep durations and patterns). For example, Hauri reports that when people have slept well they are less moody, better able to concentrate, and less tired physically.[15] This is consistent with findings that a cheerful mood increases as the length of sleep time increases from five to nine hours. However, it has been observed that the sleeper's mood deteriorates when he or she sleeps for more than nine hours at a stretch. When it is not needed, excessive amounts of sleep seem to lead to discomfort, and people complain of feeling "worn out." Subjective estimates of poor sleep, on the other hand, have been related to several factors: reduced total sleep time, longer time taken to fall asleep, less stage IV sleep, and less REM sleep. As we have already seen, poor sleep is associated with deteriorations in mood and concentration and with increased irritability. At present, the therapeutic approach to insomnia is mainly pharmacological. A psychological approach has the merit of freshness and may help to clarify some of the persistent problems. Insomnia refers either to difficulties in falling asleep or in staying asleep, or both, but subjective estimates of how long we take to fall asleep or how long we have remained asleep do not correspond closely to the facts. For example, Schwartz studied a group of patients who complained that they scarcely slept during the night. Using EEG criteria, he found that they slept throughout the greater part of the night but woke frequently for brief periods. On the following morning they claimed that they had not slept at all; their perception of the amount of sleep was grossly distorted.[16] Another common misconception of poor sleepers was described by Monroe.[17] His subjects were classified as either good or poor sleepers on the basis of the same EEG criteria. Good sleepers estimated that it took them about seven minutes to fall asleep and this was subsequently confirmed in the sleep laboratory. Poor sleepers, on the other hand, estimated that it took them just short of one hour to fall asleep. In fact it was found that they took a mere eight minutes longer than the good sleepers. However, the poor sleepers did not overestimate on every aspect of sleep and were reasonably accurate in estimating the number of times they awoke during the night. Misperceptions of the time of falling asleep and the duration of sleep are important because hypnotic drugs are prescribed in response to complaints made by patients – and in reaching their decisions about prescribing these drugs, doctors have to rely on their patient's own account of his or her sleep satisfaction.

It is possible that the misperceptions are caused in part by the heightened physiological arousal observed in poor sleepers both before sleep and early in the sleeping period. They commonly experience accelerations of heart rate, increased vasoconstriction, and higher rectal temperature. Findings of this type encourage the hope that action taken before going to sleep (such as relaxation) may help people to fall asleep more easily and to benefit from it. We already have some evidence that relaxation can be put to good therapeutic use in helping students to overcome mild insomnia (see p. 60).

The fact that at least two types of misperception concerning the extent of sleeplessness have been identified does not mean that sufferers are faking their sleep problems. Rather, it emphasizes the heterogeneity of the group of people who complain about sleeplessness. They range from people who sleep an average number of hours but underestimate the time they spend asleep or who do not feel refreshed afterwards, to those who both claim and manifest a chronic shortage of sleep. Into this latter group, fall mainly people with psychiatric complaints and the old. The importance of acknowledging this heterogeneity and identifying subtypes of insomnia has been forcefully argued by Borkovec.[3] Following earlier work, he argues for the importance of distinguishing between those whose complaint of delayed sleep onset and short sleep time is objectively corroborated and those who make identical complaints that are not corroborated. Unfortunately, this distinction between subtypes of insomnia sufferers, which also has therapeutic implications, is insufficiently recognized.

What factors determine a person's judgment of the adequacy of his or her sleep? There are the obvious ones, such as feelings of physical fatigue, discomfort in the eyes, and painful muscles upon awakening. Another important element is the person's assessment of how efficiently he or she works. Wilkinson has analyzed the ways in which performance can be impaired by varying amounts of sleep deprivation, and his findings include evidence of lapses in performance, marked by voluntary and involuntary pauses in activity.[11] This deterioration apparently can be reduced if the person is allowed to pace a task for himself, if the length of the task is shortened, or if he can be highly motivated.

An interesting determinant of sleep satisfaction, which is as obvious as it is neglected, arises from each person's belief about his or her sleep needs. We develop a conception of how much sleep we need on the basis of past experience, and our judgment of the benefit derived from any single night's sleep is made on this basis. Such evaluations of sleep are to some extent idiosyncratic. It remains to be seen if these personal conceptions are open to modification and, if so, what effects successful modification would have on sleeping habits and the benefit derived from sleep. These and the related psychological questions are intrinsically interesting and potentially useful.

Anxiety has been shown to affect both the speed of the onset of sleep and the number of awakenings during the night; these are two crucial factors in sleeplessness. There is also some indirect evidence that the reduction of anxiety facilitates improved sleep, and as we hope to show in Chapter 10, the alleviation of anxiety is the psychologist's strong hand. When psychologists turn their attention to sleep disorders, we can expect them to explore the clinical value of their anxiety-reduction methods as an early priority. It is worth bearing in mind that other states or activities that produce heightened arousal, such as concentrated study or intense physical exercise, also retard the onset of sleep. In the hands of informative general practitioners these facts can be put to clinical use simply and effectively. So, patients complaining of insomnia might be reminded to avoid drinking coffee in the evening, taught to use relaxation exercises before going to bed, and advised not to engage in intense physical or mental activities within an hour or two before retiring.

It has been claimed that stress reduces the amount of time spent in the deepest stage of sleep, which is the stage closely associated with mental and physical refreshment. This may help to explain the reported sense of fatigue following sleep taken during periods of stress. There are also data which indicate that sleep requirements change during times of stress or increased mental or physical work. At these times more sleep is needed in order to achieve comparable refreshment.

To summarize, the psychological state of the person just before sleep can lead to disturbances of the onset, continuity, and duration of sleep. And it is these characteristics that affect the sleeper's estimate of sleep satisfaction. Consequently, improved control of anxiety and avoidance of intense physical or intellectual activities just before sleep can contribute to sleep satisfaction. Modification of patients' conceptions of their sleep needs may also be of some therapeutic value.

Psychological treatments

We shall not discuss pharmacological approaches to treatment, as they have already been briefly considered. The need for other approaches arises from the problems associated with hypnotic drugs, such as dependence and rebound effects, especially when they are used over long periods. These drugs seem to be most effective when immediate results are needed, as in acute circumscribed crises rather than in chronic disorders. For less severe problems, nonpharmacological means are to be preferred. In these cases, placebos, relaxation, or repeated monotonous stimulation may suffice. Variants of relaxation, systematic desensitization, and hyponotic relaxation have been used, sometimes to good effect. For example, Borkovec and Fowles achieved some success in helping female college students with their sleeping difficulties.[18] The forty women were alloted to one of four groups: self-relaxation, therapist-administered relaxation, hypnotic relaxation, or a control group who were not treated. Each of the treated women received three therapy sessions each lasting one hour, and instructions to practice the relaxation techniques just before going to bed. All three of the treated groups reported significant improvement after therapy, whereas the women who had no treatment showed no change. In a second study, by Steinmark and Borkovec, forty-eight students with sleep problems randomly assigned to relaxation treatment, relaxation and desensitization to the state of sleep itself, placebo, or a no-treatment control. In a carefully conducted experiment they were able to conclude that all three treated groups showed significantly greater improvement than the untreated students. Relaxation therapy, with or without desensitization, proved to be particularly useful.[19] Since this early work, Borkovec and his colleagues have explored the potent element in relaxation treatment, as well as its effect on the two subtypes of insomnia (see above). Their exploration has entailed objective as well as subjective assessments of sleep loss, and elegantly designed experiments to control for the strong placebo and suggestibility effects. (The progress of the research is summarized in Borkovec's recent monograph.[3]) He has been able to pinpoint the systematic release of muscle tension as the crucial ingredient in effective treatment. This research is a good example of the impact psychology can have on theory and practice in behavioral medicine.

Psychologists can also help people who are concerned that they are getting too little sleep and who are overestimating the amount of sleep they are losing. It would be of interest, for example, to see how far judgments of sleep satisfaction can be modified by giving the person information – accurate or inaccurate – about the duration of his or her sleep. Psychologists may also be able to help in dealing with the problem of drug dependence by arranging graded and supported reductions in dosage of drugs. As an easy start, clearer information can be provided to the users of hypnotics in order to anticipate and perhaps reduce the psychological upsets experienced after withdrawal of the pills. Placebos may also be of use in this respect when dealing with mild cases of insomnia.

Case illustrations

Two cases of successful psychological modification will help to give some idea of the opportunities available. Repetitive stimulation by auditory tones was used with a fair amount of success in one of our patients. She was a young nurse who had become addicted to barbiturates in her attempts to sleep during the day when she was on night shifts. Without barbiturates she had been unable to sleep and therefore unable to work efficiently the next night. It led to her stealing drugs while on duty, and her career was in jeopardy. Following drug withdrawal, she slept, on an average, two to three hours a night, with a very late sleep onset following many anxious hours of trying to fall asleep. A treatment was developed to lower her general state of high arousal and to speed the onset of sleep. At first she was to entertain herself in pleasant but not highly stimulating tasks until about 2 A.M. Then she was to go to bed, practise her relaxation exercises, and listen to a tape of auditory signals of low intensity that were repeated every few seconds. The tape was designed to be monotonous and thereby reduce central vigilance. The patient began to fall asleep more quickly and for longer periods. With this improvement, she began her night progressively earlier. She worked back until she was sleeping six to seven hours a night from about 11 P.M. Although one might have expected a gradual recovery from the addicted state with time, it was felt that the treatment had substantially increased the rate of recovery and led to the patient sleeping even longer than she had before the night-shift disturbance.

Another patient treated by one of the authors showed an interesting relationship between her phobia and a persistent nightmare. The patient was referred for treatment of a phobia of worms and snakes that had led her to becoming virtually housebound. During the initial interview, she also complained of a disturbed sleep pattern. She frequently dreamt that she was standing on the edge of an open grave, and this repeated nightmare had disturbed her for many years.

A psychological treatment known as flooding (see Chapter 10) was used successfully to reduce the phobic reaction to worms. The patient was enabled once again to go out and about without any fears, pick up and hold worms, and so on. Toward the end of the short treatment for the phobia she reported that she was sleeping much better and had stopped dreaming of graves and coffins. Although no precise explanation could be found for the relation between the phobia and her nightmares, it is of interest that the elimination of the fear was followed by the disappearance of the nightmare. It seems possible that her considerable anxiety during the day may have persisted during sleep periods, thereby making nightmares more likely. The reduction of her anxiety was therefore followed by undisturbed sleep.

Nocturnal bed wetting

Studies of the prevalence of bed wetting (enuresis) in Britain and elsewhere uniformly show that this habit declines with age. Between 10 and 20 percent of children are still wetting at four-and-a-half years of age, but this proportion declines roughly to 5 percent by the age of nine and only 2 percent by the age of fifteen.[20] At all ages, slightly more boys than girls are bed wetters.

For a long time it was erroneously believed that bed wetting is a symptom of generalized emotional or psychiatric disorder. As numerous psychological investigations[21-25] have failed to find any significant relationship between bed wetting and maladjustment, speculations about the underlying meaning of enuresis need to be scrutinized with care. Excluding those uncommon cases in which a physical dysfunction is responsible or where there is severe psychological disturbance, bed wetting in childhood is best regarded as simply a developmental disorder. It is, incidentally, a disorder that tends to run in families. Young and Turner have estimated that in the cases of between 60 and 70 percent of children suffering from enuresis who come for professional assistance there are, or have been, other sufferers in their families.[25]

If bed wetting is not seen as a symptom of emotional disorder, psychotherapeutic treatment is unlikely to be appropriate. Contrary to the belief held by many child guidance experts, psychotherapy does not reduce bed wetting. In two investigations of this possibility, bed wetters who received psychotherapy did no better than those who received no treatment at all.[26-27] It needs to be borne in mind that it is a developmental disorder; most bed wetters will achieve continence, in time, without treatment.

It follows that the usual purpose of treatment is to expedite the natural but sometimes unacceptably slow development of continence. So far, psychological treatment has proved the most successful method of achieving this end. The bell-and-pad alarm method of conditioning treatment, in which a bell wakens the child as soon as the sheet is wet, helps to achieve continence, in roughly six to eight weeks, in approximately 70 percent of cases.[28-31] The outstanding problems with this type of treatment include the need to reduce the unacceptably large relapse rate, to improve parental cooperation, and to clarify the theoretical basis of the treatment.

Nightmares

Nightmares vary from unpleasant dreams to intense night terrors, and can be related to factors such as alcohol addiction, withdrawal from drugs, and periods of past or present stress. But this is not always so. Some people suffer from periodic or repeated nightmares for no detectable reason. Fisher and his colleagues identified three types of nightmare by relating them to the EEG activity present at the onset of the nightmare. The most intense and pathological nightmares occur not during REM periods but in stage IV, deep sleep. They start without warning and are associated with sudden, intense activity of the autonomic nervous system, including increased heart rate and respiratory rate. The sleeper does not react to external stimuli, cannot be awakened, appears mentally confused and disoriented, and is unable to recall the dream. Fisher gives this description of a typical sufferer. His nightmare began with a "sudden loud scream of blood-curdling intensity." About six out of ten of his nightmares, these outbreaks of uncontrolled anxiety, took place during the first period of non-REM sleep, after one-and-a-half hours of sleep. The subject passed instantly into a highly aroused state "in which he appeared to be dis-associated, confused, unresponsive to his environment and hallucinating. His heart rate increased within 30 seconds from 64 beats per minute to 152 beats per minute." Afterwards he could recall next to nothing of the nightmare.[32]

The second type of nightmare usually occurs during REM sleep and often is associated with anxiety dreams. In these cases, the anxiety is preceded by a more gradual increase in cardiac and respiratory activity.

In absolute terms the increase is smaller (heart rate increases of between fifteen and twenty beats per minute), but is nevertheless associated with subjective sensations of racing heart and other feelings of anxiety. On awakening this heightened physiological state reverts quickly to normal. Generally the person can recall the dream afterwards.

Finally there are nightmares that awaken sleepers from stage II sleep. These are not heralded by cardiovascular changes but do show moderate increases in heart rate following awakening (they are not nearly as intense as stage IV nightmares).

Little has been contributed from a psychological point of view to the reduction of nightmares of any variety. It seems likely that the last two types mentioned, REM and stage II dreams, can be influenced by daytime manipulations as well as by night-time inferences. Successful attempts to modify daily anxiety or stress may of course reduce the frequency or intensity of the nightmares.

In the case of recurring dreams, the formation of relevant habits might defuse the disturbing thoughts both in the day and the night. Having acknowledged that sleeping is an active process during which the mind is occupied, though in an unusual way, it would be interesting to investigate how much control a person can acquire over his "thinking" while dreaming. Is it possible to achieve a degree of self-control over the content of one's dream by conscious focusing and switching of one's thoughts, in preparation, as it were, for the night's dream-work?

Night-time "interference" refers to attempts to control nightmares by autonomic monitoring. When signs of a disturbing dream sequence begin to emerge on autonomic tracings, external stimulation could be introduced to lighten the sleep. It is hoped that this will result in an avoidance of the nightmare. The fearful stage IV nightmares, which come without warning, could not be dealt with in this way, and, in any event, excessive interference with stage IV sleep might produce problems of its own, arising out of the consequent deprivation of this type of sleep.

In concluding, we hope that the facts and notions set out here will encourage psychologists and doctors to enlarge their view of sleep problems by incorporating neglected but important psychological factors. The opportunities for expanding our comprehension of ordinary and disturbed sleep are excellent and in time will no doubt improve the range and quality of clinical help available to insomniacs and other sufferers.

7 Placebo power

The prescription of pills plays a major part in contemporary medicine. To the millions of drugs prescribed by doctors each year, we must add twice as many that are taken without prescription. We also know that crucial factors in determining and maintaining the epidemic of pill taking are psychological: Many of the effects produced by the pills are wholly psychological, others partly so. Even if psychologists restricted themselves solely to understanding the psychology of pill taking, their active participation in medical specialties additional to psychiatry would be fully justified.

It has been observed that medicine taking is a common activity, frequently indulged in, often over long periods. It serves a variety of needs, many of them social and psychological rather than purely pharmacological.[1] Extensive research has established beyond any doubt that swallowing substances of no medicinal value in the form of a pill (placebo) is capable of producing powerful psychological effects. This single fact plays a valuable part in attempts to explain the astonishing incidence of pill taking and the ever-increasing variety of pills, both prescribed and nonprescribed, available on the market. It also helps to explain why patients expect very commonly to be given pills when they pay a visit to the doctor – and in turn, it helps to account for the way in which this expectation has influenced doctors so that they prescribe pills readily and frequently. Before embarking on an examination of some of the major psychological factors that contribute to the power of placebos, it is as well to provide some facts and opinions about the pill-taking habits of patients – and the prescribing habits of doctors.

In 1967 the health authorities in Hartlepool, a small town in England, invited people to return their unused medicines, and they received no less than 43,000 tablets within one week – from only 500 homes. This is nearly ninety tablets per home. As part of the same investigation, a survey carried out in homes in the same area revealed that 94 percent of them contained some nonprescribed medicine and 29 percent of all the medicines found had been in the house for longer than a year. The researchers also estimated that roughly 6 percent of the prescribed medicines that patients have actually gone to the trouble of having made up are not used. It has been estimated that the cost of vitamin tablets to the British National Health Service amounts to several million pounds each year, and this of course does not take account of the considerably greater sums spent on purchasing proprietary preparations from pharmacies and other shops. Commenting on these habits, Dunlop points out that while vitamin supplements are desirable in the diet of pregnant women, infants, and some old people, "there is no scientific evidence that in healthy people vitamins prevent infections, stimulate appetite, help to assuage neuritic pains or aid positive health in any way." He concludes that "the wholesale consumption of vitamin concentrates... is a waste of money."[2]

As we stated earlier, Dunlop reckons that in Britain roughly one person in every ten takes a hypnotic drug, such as barbiturate, to be able to sleep. It seems that "people want to turn consciousness on and off like a tap."

One has to consider also the consequences of extensive overprescribing in producing the adverse side effects that accompany many of the most effective drugs. Wade quotes evidence to show that the more drugs a person receives, the more likely he or she is to suffer adverse reactions.[3] In one study, the proportion of adverse reactions observed in patients receiving between one and five drugs was 18 percent but rocketed to more than 80 percent in patients receiving more than five drugs simultaneously. Despite the increased risks involved and our ignorance about the synergistic effects of taking several drugs at the same time, multiple prescribing has become a common practice. In an example quoted by Dunlop, patients in a reputable hospital were found to be receiving, *on the average,* no less than fourteen drugs at the same time (small wonder that nurses have so little time to talk to their patients). None of the patients investigated in this survey had had less than six types of drugs, and one of them had received as many as thirty-two. Unwittingly perhaps, many patients have taken avoidance action. As we saw earlier, many prescriptions are not made up, and we also know that few people seem to take the tablets "as prescribed." An example of the way in which patients in a surgical ward disposed of drugs was described in Chapter 3. None of the eight pseudo-patients who simulated insanity in the study reported by Rosenhan (described below) were regarded as uncooperative.[4] Nevertheless, they managed to collect and store all the 2,000 tablets they were given in the hospital.

The other drug problem

Figures describing drug-taking habits are so astronomic as to border on the meaningless. Dunlop, for example, has calculated that in the first twenty years of the operation of the National Health Service in Britain, the drug bill increased more than fivefold.[2] Again, the number of National Health Service prescriptions rose from 206 million in 1963 to 256 million in 1972, at a cost of £211 million. In their survey of pill-taking habits, Dunnell and Cartwright found that no less than 55 percent of their respondents had taken some form of medicine in the preceding twenty- four hours; two thirds of all these medicines were not prescribed. Perhaps even more striking is the fact that 40 percent of the adults had taken some form of medicine *on each day* of the two-week period prior to the inquiry. As they point out, taking medicine is "not only a common but also a frequent activity for many people." According to the authors, most of the pills were palliative and "probably a great deal would be illogical or irrelevant in simple pharmacological terms. . . but the efficacy of medicine does not depend only on its pharmacological properties."

It is hard to tell whether the widespread prescription of drugs by doctors is a response to public demand or vice versa. Although it is true that in the Dunnell and Cartwright survey it emerged that two-thirds of all the medicines the respondents had taken were nonprescribed, this should be seen against the background of a patient's expectation from a consultation with a doctor–for the same authors found that in two-thirds of the medical consultations they studied, the doctor concluded by writing a prescription. They also learned that many doctors feel they would prescribe less if they had more time to spend with their patients. In any event, it seems that whether one visits a doctor or stays at home, the pharmaceutical industry benefits.

When does a person with a complaint stay at home and when does he visit his doctor's office? From this survey, it is clear that people seek medical advice for only a small proportion of their complaints, probably less than a third of them. It was found that although 92 percent of the adults had some symptom in a two-week period, only 16 percent had consulted their doctor. Instead, they sought advice elsewhere (commonly from a chemist) or treated themselves by medication or other means. The most common medicine taken by the respondents in the sample under description consisted of pain killers. Forty-one percent of those interviewed had taken at least one such pill in the preceding two weeks. The other popular medicines were laxatives and skin ointments. The evidence seems to suggest that self-medication is the most common alternative to visiting the doctor. There are, however, important differences of opinion both among patients and in the medical profession itself about which problems or complaints justify a visit to the doctor. Some doctors believe that the public should be encouraged to treat themselves as much as possible, whereas others hold the conservative view that patients should seek medical advice about most of their complaints.

It should not be thought that all the evidence obtained in this investigation was discouraging. Among other findings, it turned out that the majority of patients do accept their doctors' advice about what medicine to take, do get their prescriptions made up, and do use at least some of them. Some common reasons for the incorrect use of drugs–usually a failure to continue taking them for the period prescribed–include improvements of symptoms, fears of addiction, and negative attitudes toward drug taking. Another encouraging finding to emerge from this and other studies is the declining passion for laxatives. There has been a dramatic drop in the previously widespread, unwarranted, and almost daily use of laxatives.

In his passing mention of this problem, Dunlop remarks that in the earlier view of digestive troubles, the colon "was regarded as a poisonous cesspit," but now "it is more generally realized that moderate constipation constitutes a far smaller menace to health than overenthusiastic efforts to treat it."

The decline in the use of laxatives reflects a change in attitudes toward digestive processes that can be regarded as a triumph of medical education. For anyone who feels that we exaggerate, here are some selections from a well-known, popular book of medical advice published in Britain in the 1920s by Dr Robert Bell, when he was Vice-President of the International Society for Cancer Research. He was a prominent physician of his time. The quotations are taken from the fifth edition of *Woman in Health and Sickness* (1923).[5] Care of the digestive processes is given a central place in hygiene.

> Constipation is probably the most frequent source of trouble that the female has to contend with. It generally originates in carelessness and want of attention to the daily evacuation of the bowels. Mothers cannot be too particular in insisting upon their children paying a daily visit to the WC.

This advice must be adhered to because "many of the illnesses which young girls are liable to are the direct effect of neglect of this simple hygienic precaution." We cannot quote all the ills and misfortunes awaiting those foolish girls who fail to take Dr Bell's advice, but note that "some people have recourse to an aperient whenever a headache manifests itself, and as a rule they are right, because the bowels are usually at fault." Hysteria calls for a battery of remedies, and "the bowels should also be carefully regulated and pills taken regularly for two weeks." Displacement of the womb? The womb should be retained by the use of "suitable mechanical appliances," and general treatment requires that "the bowels should be carefully regulated . . . with a view of assisting the digestive process, the pills prescribed will prove very helpful." After that, the treatment of a mere inflammation of the womb is surely obvious. In addition to rest and localized treatment, this condition is treated by "a careful regulation of the bowels." Meanwhile, "to avoid varicose veins: first, attend to the daily evacuation of the bowels; second, support the pregnant womb by a well-fitting abdominal bandage; and third, do not wear garters." Finally, mothers were reminded that their sins could be transmitted to their offspring. According to Dr Bell, "Frequently we find the digestion of the infant at fault from no other cause than that the mother's digestive organs are out of order. She should therefore see that her bowels act regularly every day."

Considering the terrors of constipation in the 1920s (and it should be remembered that Dr. Bell's views were by no means unusual), who can deny the value of an educational system which has ensured that the use of laxatives failed to keep pace with the steep increase in the use of tranquillizers?

Magic pills

Large numbers of people experience powerful effects, beneficial or adverse, when they take inert substances disguised in the form of pills. The nature and determinants of the symbolic value of pill taking are preeminently psychological subjects. Although we are far from achieving a thorough understanding of placebo reactions, we do have some knowledge about the factors that influence the size, nature, and direction of such reactions.

In a recent study conducted in a general practice in South London, it was found that more than half of the forty patients receiving these inert placebos (for the reduction of anxiety) complained of unpleasant side effects.[6] One-quarter said that the pills had given them headaches, another quarter complained that the pills interfered with their sleep or their alertness. Other patients complained that they produced nausea, blurred vision, shakiness, and so on. In a second example, from the University of California, 300 neurotic patients were given one of three types of tranquillizers or an inert placebo throughout the six months of their treatment by psychotherapy. All four groups of patients showed slight improvement over the treatment period and again at a two-year follow-up inquiry. Brill and his colleagues could detect no differences between the improvements registered by the three drug-treated groups and the patients who received placebos.[7] It was also found that the effects of psychotherapy were hardly noticeable, being neither smaller nor greater than those observed in patients who had received the inert placebos.

Our third example, a study carried out on neurotic patients at the Johns Hopkins Medical School in Baltimore, produced a remarkable outcome. Park and Covi were interested in finding out how their patients would respond to a placebo when they were fully informed about its inert contents.[8] Each of the fifteen patients was assessed on his or her first visit and then given a prescription of placebo. They were also given the following explanation: "Many people with your kind of condition have also been helped by what are sometimes called "sugar pills," and we feel that a so-called sugar pill may help you too. Do you know what a sugar pill is? A sugar pill is a pill with no medicine in it at all. I think this pill will help you as it has helped so many others. Are you willing to try this pill?"

Each patient was given a supply of the inert substance in the form of pink capsules "contained in a small bottle with a label showing the name of the Johns Hopkins Hospital. He was instructed to take capsules quite regularly, one capsule three times a day at each mealtime." The researchers saw the patients a week later to reevaluate their condition and to explore their reactions to having been given a nonactive drug.

Fourteen of the fifteen patients kept their second appointment, and all but one of them took the prescribed dosage more or less as instructed. Thirteen of them showed improvement.

The magnitude of the improvement can be gauged from the fact that there was a 41 percent decrease in symptoms. Three of the patients also complained of side effects that they attributed to the action of the pills. Nine of the fourteen patients felt that the pill was "the major factor in their improvement." The most surprising feature of the result is that improvement occurred even in the patients who knew that the placebo was in fact inert. "There was no difference in improvement ratings between those eight patients who believed the pills contained placebo and the six patients who believed an active drug was involved." To cap it all, four of the fourteen patients stated that the placebo pill was "the most effective ever prescribed for them."

This particular example of placebo power cannot be attributed to mere credulity. The authors themselves attributed most of the beneficial effect to the enthusiasm with which the participant doctors carried out their task.

As it is so remarkable, this finding needs to be replicated in larger samples, including nonpsychiatric groups. As we shall see, there is independent evidence that the attitude of the prescribing doctor toward the pills and the way in which this attitude comes across to the patient are important factors in the patient's reaction to placebos. This, incidentally, is one of the main reasons for the inclusion, in strict clinical trials of drugs and other forms of treatment, of independent assessors and for keeping the participant doctors in ignorance about the tablets that they are prescribing. Failure to provide this type of "double-blind" control would mean biased procedures and assessments that would distort the interpretation of the effects of the treatment.

In an extensive review of current knowledge, one of the most prominent research workers in this field has traced the decline and fall of various medical panaceas.[9] He reminds us that Galen's elaborate book of medicines contained 820 substances – "all worthless." Nevertheless, the grand old man and his numerous disciples administered these substances in various combinations to the great satisfaction of many of their patients. Paradoxically, these physicians probably did help their patients despite the administration of useless and sometimes dangerous medications. Treatments recommended by medical authorities in a confident way that is designed to arouse hope and expectations will frequently have a beneficial outcome. All too often, however, this important factor is ignored. Doctors in particular tend to adopt a defensive position on the question of placebos instead of capitalizing on these powerful nonspecific contributors to the relief of distress. Shapiro found that whereas most physicians admit the occurrence of placebo reactions, they tend to play down their importance in their own medical speciality.[9] So "surgeons exclude surgery" from the definition of placebo, and "psychotherapists and psychoanalysts exclude psychotherapy and psychoanalysis." A greater understanding of placebo reactions would enable doctors to use them to greatest effect in their own fields.

These nonspecific, placebo reactions occur not only in drug administration but in virtually all forms of medical treatment.[10] For example, in an experimental study of the treatment of anxiety about speaking in public Paul achieved moderately good results by the skillful use of what he called an attention-placebo condition.[11] His subjects were taken to a sophisticated-looking laboratory in order to engage in a variety of meaningless tasks and measurements, carried out by an efficient and authoritative "therapist."

Premature or excessive reliance on placebo tactics is, however, inadvisable, not least because they are capable of producing adverse effects as well as benefits. As was shown in our first example, a substantial number of people complain of unpleasant side effects from taking sugar pills. Luckily, the benefits are generally greater and more extensive than the negative reactions. Contrary to the belief of many people, placebo reactions are not necessarily fleeting. In the California drug study described earlier, benefits were derived from the administration of tranquilizers or placebos, and the placebo group were found to have retained their slight improvements at the end of the two-year follow-up period.[7]

As we have already seen, the placebo effect is not necessarily eliminated when the patient is informed about its inert qualities. Another curious fact is that the administration of placebos has been found to maintain people in types of treatment other than drugs. So, for example, in using the bell-and-pad method, Turner and Young found that mothers carried out the doctor's instructions more readily if a placebo was given to the child.[12] Whether one likes it or not, many patients retain a stereotyped view of what medical treatment comprises. Advice, exercises, diets, and the rest seem not to be taken as seriously as "real medicine" – sugar-coated, encapsuled, bottled, and cryptically labeled.

A further complication lies in the fact that in the ordinary course of their work it is difficult for doctors to assess the effects of the drugs they prescribe. For example, in a study of drug effects on patients with inflammatory joint diseases, Joyce found that fifteen of the twenty patients expressed satisfaction with the phenylbutazone prescribed by Dr. B, whereas only five of eighteen of Dr. A's patients felt satisfied when given the same drug.[13] Five of Dr. C's patients were most satisfied with a placebo drug, but only one of Dr. B's patients had this reaction. Joyce notes in passing that had Dr. B not participated in this particular trial, phenylbutazone might well have been dismissed as ineffective. The major point, however, is that had they known the identity of the drugs they were using, it is likely that the three doctors particpating would have drawn very different conclusions about the effects of their prescritions. As we shall see presently, the doctor's expectation of outcome can be crucial in determining the therapeutic effects of the treatment. It comes as no surprise, then, to find that uncontrolled studies of therapeutic drug actions are claimed to be effective five times more frequently than independently assessed investigations. Foulds observed that in twenty controlled investigations of therapeutic drug action, success was claimed in only five of them; in fifty-two uncontrolled studies, however, claims of successful drug action were made in forty-three of the fifty-two studies.[14]

The important part played by the doctor's expectations of success or failure is neatly illustrated in a report by Uhlenhuth and others.[15] Two psychiatrists who differed in their expectations of drug effects were asked to prescribe drugs and placebos to their patients. The patients of the optimistic doctor responded substantially better than did those of the sceptical doctor. The manner in which the doctor introduces and recommends the pills to the patient is certainly influential in producing the resulting drug effect. On a more mandane level, reactions to drugs have been found to be susceptible to such superficial characteristics as the color of the tablets, whether they are pills or capsules, the nature of the instructions for administering them, and so on. We also know that certain types of people are more likely to react to placebo treatment than others. In medical and surgical patients, as well as in psychiatric patients, placebo responses are more common in sociable, conventional, dependent people, whereas mistrustful and isolated patients tend to show little or no placebo reaction. Anxious patients are more likely to show placebo reactions than nonanxious ones.

An important aspect of the doctor's "placebo power" is the amount of personal interest he shows in his patient. This is likely to be associated with the patient's liking for him and hence of the patient's tendency to comply with the doctor's advice and to find his prescriptions to be effective. Doctors who show little personal interest in their patients are seldom liked by them, and their "placebo power" is diminished.

The doctor's enthusiasm for the treatment he is recommending appears to enhance its value. This enthusiasm, which has obvious advantages, helps to explain why the innovators of new forms of treatment so often obtain better results than anyone else. Enthusiasm of this kind is probably at the bottom of another interesting therapeutic phenomenon – novel treatments are often found to be more effective than older forms. It is for this reason that doctors are sometimes given the half-serious advice to "use a new form of treatment while it works."

The occurrence of placebo reactions is usually regarded as a source of embarrassment. They can, however, be turned to advantage and used to make treatment and care more resourceful and effective. Recognition of the pervasiveness of placebo effects is a first step in this direction. In time, psychological research will improve our understanding of their nature and enable us to exploit them sensibly. We need not continue to use placebos in the present restricted manner–that is, mainly to provide a safe basis for comparison with new drugs and other treatments. With little extra effort we can increase the power of our pills (and our doctors) by skillful boosting of those qualities and factors that make a nonspecific (placebo) contribution to therapy, such as the enthusiasm of doctors and the confidence of patients.

All this calls for greater concentration on psychological factors. The primary need is for intensive research, mainly of a psychological character, into the *determinants* of placebo phenomena. It is essential that this research is broadened to include specialties outside psychiatry. In our view, attention should be shifted toward general-practice medicine and to the selection and effects of nonprescribed medicines.

8 Self-control of bodily functions

Control yourself

When our bodily discomforts or pains reach an intense level, we generally seek the advice of people we are close to, usually friends and relatives. Depending on their reactions, and our discomforts, we then might seek the advice of a doctor. Alternatively, we might decide to do nothing, or try a self-selected medicine, or change our behavior. This last alternative covers a range of possible actions – taking a rest, drinking less alcohol, eating less (or more), getting more sleep, exercising, changing diets, moving house, or simply thinking healthy thoughts. Another important possibility, that of changing our behavior in order to increase *direct* bodily control, has not been taken seriously until recently. Advancing psychological research has shown that, given appropriate training conditions, we are capable of achieving partial control of bodily functions (e.g., heart rate) that were formerly regarded as being entirely involuntary. Given the necessary support and some good fortune, psychologists may soon find themselves in possession of techniques for improving bodily self-control – for example, to reduce pain. We may yet see the return, in modern dress, of that popular Victorian prescription – "Exercise self-control."

Another old saying, "Know thyself," may also take on amusing new significance as psychologists begin to pay attention to the individual's *internal* environment. We can expect improvements in our sensitivity to internal events and an expansion of language, made necessary by the need to communicate our internal sensations more precisely and effectively. In time, these scientific advances will influence medical practice – most obviously because the patient's account of his or her internal sensations and events is the basis of clinical practice.

Some Western doctors and psychologists also have a new interest in acupuncture (particularly in relation to pain) and in meditation. The interest in meditation is more than a romantic longing; it arises from two significant advances made by experimentalists working in the mainstream of psychological research. In the first place, research by Neal Miller and his colleagues has shown that certain functions of the autonomic nervous system, formerly thought to be beyond deliberate control, can be manipulated with some accuracy by the actions of the organism concerned. So, for example, a rat can be taught to increase the vasomotor responses of its left ear while those of its right ear continue unchanged.[1] The second and related advance comes from experimental attempts to train people to attain a measure of voluntary control over some of their own bodily functions, such as heart rate. The research directed at increasing self-control relies mainly on a technique called *biofeedback*.

The term refers to procedures in which biological information about a person's functions are "fed back" to him by technical devices that provide him with an external display of his internal functions, for example, a second-by-second visual display of his heart rate. This biological information is, of course, inaccesible under ordinary circumstances and is displayed externally in order to give the patient the means to control aspects of his bodily functions that are otherwise independent of his direct control. The functions that have attracted most attention are heart rate, blood pressure, and electrical activity in the brain (EEG) and of the skin, all of which have long been regarded, at least in the West, as being involuntary. It has now been established that under specified conditions, a person who is provided with feedback about certain of his bodily functions can learn to control them to some extent.

An example will clarify the procedure. In order to teach a person how to achieve a measure of control over her heart rate, electrodes are attached to her body and connected to a pulse meter, so that a continuous measure of her heart rate is obtained. This measure is then translated into a visual signal from which she is able to observe the speed of her heart rate, second by second, or beat by beat. She is instructed to use this normally inaccessible information in order to increase or decrease the rate. In some instances she need be given no further information than that simple instruction. More efficient control can be achieved by providing her with some hints, such as the fact that imagining exciting activities will facilitate heart rate increases and imagining calm and drowsy situations will tend to slow it down. Figure 3 shows how simple the principle of the procedure is. Improvements can be made in the form in which the feedback is presented, in the setting, or in the instructions, and so forth, but biofeedback procedures are basically rather simple.

Research on the clinical application of biofeedback training procedures is beginning to flourish. The training has the particularly attractive feature of teaching the patient how to do something for himself.[2] Some promising early results have been achieved in cases of hypertension, migraine, muscle-contraction headaches, and other problems. However, a laboratory-produced effect is only the first step – albeit an essential one – in the search for a therapeutic procedure. We are still some dis-

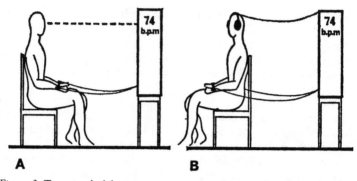

Figure 3 Two simple laboratory arrangements for training subjects to acquire control of cardiac rate. In the first (A), the subject's cardiac rate is fed into a visual display and she is instructed to increase or decrease her "score." In the second (B), her cardiac rate is transformed into an auditory signal which informs her of increases and decreases. Limited short-term changes can be obtained easily, but substantial and/or enduring changes are more difficult to achieve.

tance from establishing the latter. Miller wisely cautions against the widespread and unevaluated application of biofeedback at this early stage of its development.

Two important influences have stimulated the interest in and the application of biofeedback.

1. The first influence came from research workers who were intrigued by the self-control apparently achieved during meditation. It is held that during transcendental meditation, the monk or yogi attains voluntary control over many aspects of his bodily functions that are ordinarily inaccessible. Wenger and Bajchi, for example, described the case of a yogi who was able to perspire from his forehead on command. Another yogi could slow his heart rate to such an extent that little blood was being pumped and no heart sounds could be heard, even with a stethoscope.[3] Many other remarkable examples are quoted by Arthur Koestler in his book on India and Japan, *The Lotus and the Robot.*[4] They include some little-known instances of precise control of highly specific digestive functions, achievements that might strike Westerners as being both astonishing and pointless, in equal measure.

Apparently, experienced practitioners of meditation are capable of drawing air into their intestines by voluntary contraction of the anal sphincter. And water can be drawn in through the rectum. Altogether, Koestler found that many yogis have an obsessional interest in bowels, which probably commended them to members of the British Empire, such as Dr. Bell, as being proper and worthy.

2. The second influence came from a number of psychologists, most notably Neal Miller, who successfully challenged some firmly held beliefs about the capacities of the nervous system. For many years authorities on psychology distinguished between two types of learning and two parts of the nervous system. It was believed that the autonomic nervous system and the central nervous system mediated different types of learning. In brief, the argument went as follows: Trial-and-error learning, sometimes called instrumental learning, is mediated by the central nervous system, and the responses involved are under voluntary control. In contrast, responses mediated by the autonomic nervous system are involuntary and can be learned only by classical conditioning, a form of learning by association.

Belief in the existence of these two basic types of learning was so strong that workers such as Miller found it difficult to obtain funds and research equipment to examine alternative theories:

> The belief that is is impossible for the stupid autonomic nervous system to exhibit the more sophisticated instrumental learning was so strong that for more than a decade it was extremely hard for me to get any students or even paid assistants to work seriously on the problem. I almost always ended up by letting them work on something they did not think was so preposterous. [5]

In fact, when the experiments (on animals) were attempted, they began to achieve striking successes in training autonomic responses by instrumental learning techniques. Although the size of the controlled adjustments achieved by workers in other laboratories were smaller than and less dramatic than those obtained in the earliest experiments, they were nevertheless significant. These remarkable results prompted other experimenters to show that when *people* are given information about the activity of some aspects of their autonomic nervous system and instructed to vary that activity in order to achieve some reward, these people achieve a degree of control over their autonomic activities, for instance, increasing control over their heart rate. Thus it appears that, contrary to long-held beliefs, responses mediated by this branch of the nervous system can be manipulated, even voluntarily, after a course of training in trial-and-error learning.

Arguments about the relation between types of learning and types of nervous system are of minor interest to clinicians, however. For them it is not so much a question of the types of learning operating, as one of gaining control of previously "mute," independent response systems.

Recent research has yielded information about the factors that appear to be important to the success of biofeedback training procedures. It appears, not surprisingly, that the more accurate and more extensive the information provided to the person about the activity of the response system in question, the greater the degree of control achieved. Peter Lang, of the University of Wisconsin, has demonstrated that the provision of continuous precise feedback information facilitates the learning of heart rate control – and he is now able to train subjects to regularly achieve increases of as much as thirty beats per minute.[6-8] He has also found that learning to speed up one's heart rate is easier, and possibly different in critical respects, from learning to slow it down.

There are also data to suggest that the modality of feedback signals can affect the rate of success. Thus, for example, it has been found that an auditory feedback signal is more effective than a visual signal in lowering forehead muscle tension. The greater the enlightenment given to the person about the significance of the feedback and his reactions to it, the better the outcome. Early fears that people might perform less well when they are made aware of the purpose of the training have fortunately not been confirmed. The complexity and the power of these verbal instructions to affect visceral behavior are the subject of an interesting analysis by Professor Brener of Hull University.[9, 10]

Animal studies

Some of the most productive experimental work has come from Professor Miller's own laboratory. Operating under highly controlled laboratory conditions, learned control of diverse glandular and visceral responses has been achieved. Functions such as heart rate, intestinal motility, blood pressure, skin temperature, urine formation, and so on, have been successfully modified. Most of the research has been carried out on rats, and it was thought to be necessary to use the drug curare to paralyze temporarily the skeletal muscles in order to rule out the possible influence of muscle activities. This experimental control is coupled with the use of electrical stimulation of the reward centers of the brain, thereby allowing the experimenter to control directly the rewards given to the animal, contingent upon the occurrences of the appropriate bodily reaction (for example, an increase or decrease of heart rate). Some of the more remarkable successes included the following experiments. In one instance, heart rate and intestinal contractions were recorded in a group of rats. Half of the rats were rewarded for changes in heart rate and the other half for changes in intestinal contractions. As can be seen in Figure 4, the group rewarded for heart rate increases learned to increase the rate,

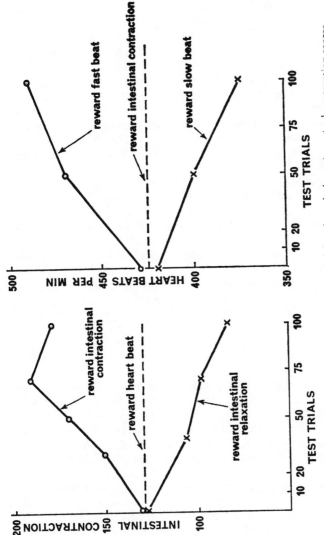

Figure 4 *The specificity of learned visceral responses.* The left-hand graph shows intestinal contraction scores. These are seen to increase or decrease in response to rewards given contingent on the occurrence of the desired intestinal responses. When heart rate changes were rewarded, no changes in intestinal contractions occurred. The right-hand graph shows the results obtained from rewarding heart rate increases or decreases. The rewarding of intestinal changes produced no alterations in heart rate. Adapted from N. E. Miller, *Science*, 163, 436 (1969).

whereas the group rewarded for intestinal contractions learned to increase this activity. The specificity of the training effect is shown by the fact that the group rewarded for heart rate increases showed no change in intestinal activity, and similarly, the group rewarded for changes in intestinal contractions showed no change in cardiac activity.

Recently Miller has reported some failures to replicate the early experiments on the control of heart rate, which were carried out in collaboration with Di Cara.[11] Although heart rate changes can be induced, they are much smaller in magnitude than those reported four to five years earlier. Miller has explored some explanations, but the reasons for the relative failure of these replications are still not clear. Recently he observed that because of failures to replicate, it is "prudent not to rely on any of the experiments in curarized animals."[2] There is nevertheless ample evidence of the learned modification of visceral responses in normal animals, in Miller's and other laboratories.[12] Even if the size of these changes turns out to be more modest than at first appeared to be the case, we can no longer view the glands and viscera as being entirely "autonomous" and quite beyond the direct control of the brain. Even extremely subtle and highly specific responses can be modified, provided that the physiological changes can be monitored and relayed back to the organism, either directly or indirectly.

Whatever the final outcome of these intensive investigations on laboratory animals, it is indisputable that this research has prompted some significant advances in our knowledge about the scope of self-control of bodily functions.

Human studies

Since the publication of Miller's early results, there have been a large number of attempts to achieve comparable results with (noncurarized) human subjects. Although some degree of self-control has been achieved over a number of responses such as gastrointestinal contractions, muscle contractions, skin temperature, and so on, most of the effort has been directed at achieving control of various aspects of the cardiovascular system. We can try to summarize a great deal of progress on controlling the heart rate, in this way. Using appropriate biofeedback techniques, it is possible to increase heart rate by an average of ten beats per minute, and some experimenters such as Peter Lang are now finding it comparatively easy to get normal subjects to increase their heart rate by by fifteen or thirty beats per minute.[8] An elevation in heart rate has turned out to be easier to achieve than a decrease in rate. Instructions to control heart rate, particularly when combined with biofeedback equipment, are a surprisingly powerful mediating force in controlling heart rate. There are individual differences in the ability to achieve control over heart rate, and these appear not to be normatively distributed in population. In particular, it seems probable that people who have had cardiovascular illnesses or difficulties are less able to gain control. On the other hand, there are some people who acquire great competence in the skill with relative ease – Lang has taken to calling them "autonomic athletes."[13] He has also found that under high incentive conditions some of his subjects can accelerate their heart rates to as high as 150 beats per minute; but as Headrick and others found earlier,[14] when one's heart rate is accelerated in this way it commonly gives rise to feelings of uneasiness and tension.

Concentrating on the learned control of blood pressure, Shapiro and his colleagues have demonstrated small but significant increases and decreases in both systolic and diastolic blood pressure under feedback arrangements.[15, 16] These changes occur independently of heart rate changes. Recently they succeeded in demonstrating that people can learn to produce integrated changes in blood pressure and heart rate if reward is provided whenever both responses occur simultaneously. Even more striking, they have also produced nonintegrated changes in which blood pressure and heart rate are made to vary independently.

Equivocal results have emerged from attempts to achieve self-control of electrodermal fluctuations (changes in the electrical resistance of the skin), perhaps because of the considerable methodological problems involved in working with this fragile measure.[17] Although the self-control of most skeletal muscles has never been at issue, the voluntary control of the basic unit of motor control (comprising an effector neuron and the attached muscle fibers) was thought to be unattainable. It has now been achieved by the use of biofeedback techniques. Basmajian has shown that under suitable feedback conditions, a person can learn sufficient control to allow him or her to generate rhythmic firing and drum-beat rhythms of one of these discrete motor units.[18]

Basmajian has also reported another surprising finding – one with clinical implications. He found that with the help of feedback procedures, absolute levels of muscle action potential can be made to drop very close to zero levels – or no muscle tension at all. This strengthens the belief that conditions in which heightened tension is implicated (and there are many of them, e.g., back pain, headaches, etc.) may respond to muscle relaxation training, using either conventional or biofeedback methods.

Electrical activity of the brain, particularly the alpha band of wave activity (eight to thirteen cycles per second), has also been modified by the use of biofeedback techniques. This alpha band occurs in states of relaxed wakefulness, and is most pronounced when the eyes are closed. It appears that people can learn to increase alpha activity or suppress it at will, irrespective of whether their eyes are open or closed.[19] These findings aroused interest among psychologists, not only because of the demonstration of specific learned control of such a complex neurophysiological process, but also because it was hoped that they might lead to a new approach to the study of mood.

The excitement unfortunately led some writers to speculate rather unwisely about what might be achieved. It was suggested, for example, that one might be able to change mood states by having a subject "turn on" a certain cerebral rhythm. It is surely misleading to conclude, as Maslow has done, that we can now "teach people how to feel happy and serene."[20] These exaggerated claims are unfounded, not least because it is unlikely that gross changes in the electrical wave activity of the brain (EEG) can ever reflect the myriad subjective moods.

In summary, even though the achievements are more modest than some people would like to believe, it is reasonable to conclude that biofeedback techniques can be used to achieve a measure of self-control over what were previously believed to be fully autonomous bodily functions. This discovery may not be news in Benares, but it generates enthusiasm in San Francisco and it may soon be put to clinical use. Learned changes in visceral responding can be achieved. We now need to find how to increase their magnitude and durability, and progress will depend on gaining some understanding of the processes involved.

Clinical applications

It is hoped that these techniques may ultimately become useful tools in the treatment of psychosomatic disorders, as well as chronic conditions such as cardiac dysfunctions, high blood pressure, headaches, and so on. Significant feedback affects have been obtained in laboratories, but can they be reproduced in a clinical setting? Might not the existing abnormality of function interfere with the capacity to acquire skill in modifying the disorder? Can we induce changes large enough to produce clinically significant improvement? In sum, can we made the transition from trivial and transient laboratory changes to substantial, enduring clinical improvement?

The novelty and appeal of the idea of biofeedback generated a great deal of enthusiasm and excessive optimism. More recently, psychologists have adopted higher critical standards and a more realistic expectation of what can be achieved. In evaluating the early results, insufficient consideration was given to those nonspecific factors (e.g., suggestion, spontaneous fluctuations, etc.) that contribute significantly to the observed effect. [21]

Engel and Weiss tried to obtain a significantly improved control of irregularities of heart beat (cardiac arrhythmia) in a group of eight patients suffering from a specific dysfunction of the heart (premature ventricular contractions). [22] The results showed some striking changes in electrocardiographic patterns (ECG) during the sessions, and all the patients gained some control over their heart rate. After a control period, all patients taught heart rate acceleration followed by deceleration, finishing off with a number of sessions in which they were taught to alternate increases and decreases of heart rate within a circumscribed period. All the patients had to maintain their heart rate within a certain range, and the feedback arrangement ensured that they knew whenever they exceeded or failed to reach the range. Five of the eight showed a more regular heart beat on at least one of the three training conditions, and four of the five were able to maintain these changes after the experiment. One patient even succeeded in retaining his new skill for as long as twenty-one months. In a recent review, Engel confirms his earlier results that heart rate can be brought under stimulus control. [23]

The application of biofeedback techniques to the lowering of systolic blood pressure in patients with hypertension has also been fruitful. [24] The results show learned decreases in blood pressure in six of the seven patients, but the changes were not consistently associated with slowing of the heart rate. As hypertension is more closely associated with *diastolic* blood pressure, the recent study by Elder and his colleagues, in which some control of diastolic pressure was achieved, encourages the hope that successful clinical applications will be possible. [25] Although most studies report significant decreases in blood pressure, few report clinically important results. Adequate follow-up data are rarely provided. The findings are sufficiently encouraging to warrant the necessary controlled trials in which the practicality of this approach to hypertension can be assessed against the usual pharmacological and alternative behavioral techniques (relaxation, meditation).

Another valuable application of biofeedback was started by Budzynski and his colleagues. [26, 27] They have been attempting to control tension headaches by training their patients to relax their muscles. These headaches are assumed to result from sustained contractions of neck and scalp muscles (see Chapter 5). In their study, the frontalis muscle alone was monitored, presumably because they assumed that this muscle was involved in the headaches experienced by all their patients. In fact, they found that the basal levels of muscle tension were exceptionally high in the headache group, equal to nearly twice that of healthy people. [More recent findings indicate that this conclusion will have to be qualified (see Chapter 5).] In a controlled treatment trial, biofeedback training involving the frontalis muscle was compared to pseudo-training in which the auditory information relayed to the patient was unrelated to the actual state of tension in the frontalis muscle. A third group of patients, receiving no relevant treatment, was also included for purposes of comparison. Significant reductions in muscle-tension levels and in headache activity were achieved by the group of patients who received the biofeedback training, and no significant improvements were observed in either of the comparison groups. The difference between the groups was still present at the three-month follow-up period. This work marked an important beginning in the management of an extremely common disorder, by methods other than drugs, and it was followed by a spurt of work on the subject that aroused a good deal of fresh interest in the subject of migraine and tension headaches.

Induced changes during biofeedback – in EMG as in blood pressure and heart rate studies – tend to be viewed as direct consequences of the feedback provided. It is argued that the patients learn self-control via the information provided. Unfortunately, few researchers check this assumption. At present, it appears more likely that other factors (e.g., general relaxation, adaptation, etc.) are operating. The exploitation of these factors – as well as the biofeedback loop – may be more fruitful in the obtaining of therapeutic changes. In tension headache, general relaxation training appears to be as potent as the specific and costly muscular training.[28] Although many studies of biofeedback for headache are available, none has shown the reduction to be associated with learned control of the muscle, demonstrated without the aid of feedback. A biofeedback approach to vascular headaches has also begun with attempts to control finger temperature as well as temporal artery pulse.[29]

As it is unlikely that the stress conditions considered to be instrumental in producing tension headaches can ever be eliminated, the introduction of methods that give the person a degree of self-control over the accumulation of tension, and hence a means of reducing the pain, is particularly welcome.

Yet another interesting application of biofeedback methods was reported by Jacob and Felton, who worked with ten patients suffering from injuries of upper trapezius muscle (see Figure 2).[30] They compared this group with ten physically normal people, and found that their injured group had a greatly heightened basal level of muscular tension and appeared to be unable to relax the trapezius muscle by ordinary means.

When provided with a visual feedback display of the activity of the muscle (myoelectric impulses) on an oscilloscope, a remarkable change occurred. Under instructions to relax, the tension levels of the patients dropped rapidly to those of the uninjured group. No information on the subjective effects experienced by the patients after such a marked change was supplied, nor can we be sure of the durability of the changes. Nonetheless, we can take seriously the challenge that these results are promising for rehabilitation and training programs in which interfering muscle groups retard corrective progress. Nor is it impossible to imagine the successful application of these techniques in helping some patients to regain at least partial use of impaired muscles.

It can be seen that a useful start has been made in applying biofeedback techniques to medical problems, but the theoretical and practical problems should not be underestimated.

Outstanding issues

At this point in a rapidly expanding field such as biofeedback, it is worth delineating some of the issues that need to be clarified, in both the laboratory and the clinic. So far, several research workers have been concerned mainly with demonstrating the acquisition of learned control, over relatively few trials and usually within a single training session. The magnitude of the effect in humans has been less important than its occurrence. The aim has been to obtain effects significantly greater than those observed in an appropriately chosen control group (for example, those who receive either no feedback at all, or incorrect feedback). However, there is no longer any doubt that these bodily systems can be modified and that feedback arrangements provide a simple and effective basis for modification. The outstanding problems are how to achieve the best conditions for encouraging self-control, how to enlarge the changes, and how to retain control even after the withdrawal of the external feedback signals.

With regard to the first issue, experiments need to be performed in which the length of both the trials themselves and the intervals between them are systematically varied. It would also be helpful if experimental reports provided more detail than simple average effects, as these data sometimes obscure important information about who is responding and how. For research aimed at clarifying the mechanisms of change, fine-grain analyses of the performance of each subject are essential. We also need systematic investigations of the effects of varying amounts and types of feedback infromation. As mentioned earlier, the type of feedback provided – visual or auditory – may also be a factor worth consideration, as people almost certainly differ in the way that they can best take in information about their own bodies. And it is essential to bear in mind that the provision of full and detailed instructions facilitates learning and is not merely a tedious duty, as was originally supposed.

The question of the durability of the effects is of central interest, especially in applications to medical problems. The aim would be to teach a lasting skill that can be used whenever the need arises. To date, little attention has been given to promoting *and testing* for effects that persist after training sessions. Such factors as the number of trials, the number of sessions, and the importance of instructions are obviously relevant and will need detailed study. It may also be that greater skill can be attained by teaching patients to "turn on" their control skills in the face of either imaginary stresses or of graded presentations of stressful material. In other words, the desensitization approach that has proved to be so useful in psychiatric application might be reshaped to teach self-control in precisely those situations of stress where it is ordinarily difficulty to apply. This is a move from a concern for control of basal states to a greater concern for control over responses during stress.

As we have seen, most of our knowledge derives from the laboratory, and there is always some doubt about the feasibility of transfer to the clinical situation. Although it may turn out that it is easier for clinical groups to decrease some abnormally elevated functions, because there is more room for change than is the case in a normally functioning group, the recent findings of Lang, referred to above, are a warning that certain disordered functions are bound to prove less amenable to training. As yet, it is too early to decide which dysfunctions are most easily modified. We have good reason to expect that there are large individual differences in subjective estimates of pain and of tension, the amount of change detectable by different subjects, and the amount of change needed to modify the symptoms.

The growth of biofeedback techniques was made possible by the development of equipment that adequately senses, amplifies, and projects the activity of biological systems. So progress will depend in part on the efficiency, size, and mobility of this equipment. On grounds of the research information accumulated so far, we can foresee the need for some patients to be provided with portable miniature systems that can be used whenever needed in daily life, to ensure that the therapeutic changes do not fade after treatment.

A great deal of work needs to be undertaken in order to develop biofeedback into practical clinical procedures. And this branch of clinical psychology alone could comfortably absorb the efforts of an entire year's crop of graduates.

Suitable medical problems

It is easy to overestimate the value of a new technique, and there is a general tendency to recommend new methods for old ailments. Even at this early stage it is worth trying to clarify the types of disorder that seem to us best suited to a biofeedback approach.

The most appropriate and most clear-cut use of biofeedback is in the modification of disorders of function that are (1) localized by specific complaints, (2) objectively quantifiable, and (3) under minimal, if any, control by the sufferer. This definition includes a range of medical problems. Suitable examples include muscular disorders such as tension headaches, low back pain, and specific motor disabilities. It might be predicted that migraine could be investigated and possibly treated by modifying the construction of dilation of arteries. Psychosomatic disorders such as ulcers might be ameliorated by teaching control of acidity level in the stomach, or, more simply, by reducing stomach tension levels. Subject to technical advances, asthma might be modified by teaching control of bronchial constriction and dilation. Some cardiovascular conditions have already received attention, and the technique looks particularly promising for people suffering from hypertension. For children suffering from hypertension, the advantages of achieving an improvement in their health by means of acquired self-control, rather than by resorting to a life-long regime of daily drug taking, are obvious.

A second major use for biofeedback techniques is in the production of changes in general state – in the hope that they will act to inhibit certain chronic complaints. As these changes in general state are ordinarily outside voluntary control, chronic sufferers might be helped if they could learn to turn on alternative states, such as deep relaxation, by making use of feedback from one or more bodily systems. As most medical disorders are of the chronic type, the case for exploring the value of biofeedback techniques in reducing these persisting discomforts and pain is a strong one.

Finally, it may turn out that the biofeedback methodology will prove more valuable for investigating the nature of psychosomatic and related disorders than for induction of therapeutic changes. As a pointer in this direction, attempts to reduce tension headache by biofeedback revealed that a sizable proportion of sufferers do *not* display excessive muscular tension, as is widely assumed (see Chapter 5).

9 Reducing health risks by self-control

Psychological factors play a large part in overeating and smoking, both forms of behavior that carry health risks. Contrary to what we often prefer to believe, smoking is not a "minor vice" but a potentially lethal form of behavior.[1] Excessive eating is also more hazardous than is generally realized.[2] In theory, both types of behavior are open to modification by psychological means. In practice, it is sad to admit, psychologists have not reported satisfactory progress in spite of the intense research conducted over the last few years. If they fail in their attempts to modify these forms of immoderate behavior, the credibility of their claims for a larger role in health services, as argued in this book, and elsewhere, will suffer. Psychologists need to do better, but can they? In this chapter we discuss some of the methods explored, the reasons for their relative failure, and the likelihood of future success.

We can anticipate one of our arguments by stating that psychologists are already in a position to achieve partial, but useful and fairly prompt success by the introduction of a new tactic. Instead of devoting all their efforts to changing the behavior of smokers, psychologists could redirect their aim and spend more time attempting to change the behavior of doctors. In this way, they could help to achieve great benefits in the short term. Although our recommendation would have no effect on resistant smokers, who either cannot or will not respond to simple measures, there is good reason to suppose that a large number of smokers would be helped. Here are our reasons for advocating this redistribution of effort. In Chapter 2 we pointed out that there will never be an adequate number of psychologists to justify clinical work based exclusively on person-to-person interactions. We need to develop methods of psychological action that are applicable on a group basis. The problem of smoking provides one such excellent opportunity. Any psychological technique for reducing smoking that is applicable only on a one-to-one basis, no matter how successful, would make little impact on the problem–bearing in mind that a majority of adults smoke. Most psychological methods of control can, of course, be modified for group application. In the case of smoking, however, an even more economical use of psychological expertise would involve changing the behavior of the doctors.

According to survey findings, only 20 percent of patients report that their doctors have ever advised them to give up smoking.[3,4] We also know from Russell's review that a doctor's advice is one of the most effective means of persuading smokers to abstain.[5] Consequently, if psychologists used their skills in persuading doctors to always give such advice, and guide them as to the most effective content and style of such advice, they would more than earn their keep.

It will be objected that the second part of this suggestion begs the question. What constitutes "effective content and style" of persuasive medical advice against smoking? Although we acknowledge the difficulty, it is our opinion that if the problems are stated in this novel way they are more likely to yield solutions. As we shall see, the main thrust of psychological research has been toward the direct modification of the smoker's behavior. We known of no systematic attempts to change the practices of doctors, and there has been insufficient interest in how and why their advice can be so successful.

If the question is asked why *psychologists* are needed to put this proposal into action, the reply is double-barrelled. In the first place, despite the many campaigns against smoking and the vast number of medical articles on the subject, only 20 percent of the patients who responded in the survey mentioned above had been advised by their doctors to give up smoking. Presumably this implies that even if we assume that all practising doctors are aware of the medical risks involved in continuous smoking (and we can safely make this assumption), for some undetected reasons this knowledge has not changed their behavior toward their patients to any marked degree. Secondly, the delivery and evaluation of persuasive communications fall within the province of psychology. Although the subject needs a great deal of development, we have some facts and findings that would be helpful in any attempt to persuade doctors to advise against smoking (see Chapter 3).

In the longer term, we need to increase our understanding of the nature and causes of smoking and to develop practical and effective treatment methods, particularly for those patients who cannot or will not respond to their doctor's advice or who relapse after a period of abstinence.

Russell, among others, has forcefully put the case that smoking should be regarded as a form of drug dependence and accordingly treated with the same degree of seriousness.[5, 6] It is pointed out that the two most worrying groups of drug-dependent people, alcoholics and drug addicts, include an extraordinarily high proportion of smokers: 99 percent of drug addicts and 92 percent of alcoholics – as opposed to 56 percent in the general population. Similarities are shown between the consequences of withdrawal from smoking and withdrawal from these other two main types of drug dependence. In all three cases it is followed by psychological distress and physiological disturbance, including sleep disorders and cardiovascular disruptions. Moreover, the relapse rates in all three types of dependence follow the same pattern.

Smoking usually starts in a social setting, before the age of twenty, and if an adolescent smokes only three or four cigarettes it is more or less certain that he will continue to smoke for several decades. The point is made dramatically by Russell:

> In the prevailing social climate it is only intravenous drugs which have anything like the dependence-producing potential of cigarette smoking, and it may be no coincidence that the absorption of nicotine through the lungs during smoking is about as rapid and efficient as the junkie's fix.[6]

Apparently the four most important influences on those starting to smoke are the number of one's friends who do so, permissive parental attitudes toward smoking, desire for adulthood, and an absence of fear of getting lung cancer. Although the large majority of smokers express the desire to cut down or cut out their smoking, only a small percentage (roughly 18 percent) achieve success. The successful abstainers tend to be over the age of thirty and have fears about their health. Among the large number of those who attempt to give up, 37 percent relapse within one year, but those who persist for two years stand roughly a three-in-four chance of succeeding. The overall tendency is for former smokers, whether treated or not, to relapse. Although three-quarters of all smokers express a desire to stop, less than one-quarter succeed in achieving their aim.

Psychological research into the factors that encourage a smoker to continue has uncovered some interesting information. Even though the *physiological* effects of smoking are stimulating, many smokers experience and report a calming *psychological* effect. There is evidence that smoking induces not only calmness but can also help to dampen some of the unpleasant psychological feelings experienced during stress. These findings are consistent with the observation that long-term smokers were more anxious during early adulthood than nonsmokers.[7] An elaborate argument relating smoking to personality has been developed by Eysenck.[8] Starting from the premise that extraverts suffer from underarousal of the cortex, he links this major dimension of personality to the arousing effects of smoking. The deduction that extraverts are more likely than introverts to be continuous smokers has been confirmed–they apparently derive satisfying increases in central stimulation from smoking. As smoking is also capable of producing the calming psychological effects referred to earlier, a proportion of the overaroused introverts also smoke. In sum, Eysenck argues that smoking is "maintained because it is an artificial aid in producing a preferred level of arousal."

Medical and other assistance

Antismoking campaigns have had little permanent success, but distinct, although brief, reductions in cigarette consumption do occur in the wake of almost all campaigns. One of the few exceptions to the general observation that the effects of these campaigns are transitory is the example of British doctors who achieved a permanent decrease in cigarette consumption, and in the prevalence of smoking, since the publication of the report on smoking by the Royal College of Physicians. Antismoking treatment provided at special clinics tends to produce an immediate success rate of anything from 30 to 85 percent, but this is quickly followed by wholesale relapse. Thus, with few exceptions the effects of clinic interventions are transitory. Commenting on the failure of the pharmaceutical profession to provide an adequate antismoking drug, Bernstein deplores the "dismal picture presented by lobeline research," the most widely recommended and used form of antismoking drug.[9]

Persistent smokers have been subjected to many different experiments designed to help them overcome the habit, but with relatively little success. These methods, which range from role-playing to aversion therapy, produce similar results–comparable to those achieved by sugar pills. None achieves more than a temporary reduction in smoking. The use of behavioral self-control techniques and of contracting programs have been a little disappointing. (The results of a large study on 416 smokers counselled by ten psychologists at the Max Planck Institute in Munich, under the direction of Dr. Brengelmann, offer some encouragement. The best results were achieved with self-control programs and aversion therapy, alone or in combination.) Nor have methods designed to change attitudes been as effective as had been hoped; they have, incidentally, helped to confirm that even when the smoker's attitude is successfully changed, he will not necessarily change his behavior accordingly, if at all.[10] Nor indeed is a favorable change in attitude a prerequisite for satisfactory change in behavior. It is dispiriting to have to report that the small successes that have been achieved in applying psychological methods of control to smoking are of the aversive type. The administration of mild to moderate electric shocks to patients at various points in the chain of smoking behavior was reasonably successful in Russell's pilot study,[11] carried out on fourteen smokers referred from a clinic dealing with chest ailments. Application of the electrical aversion method produced a rapid reduction in smoking in the majority of patients and long-term abstention in six of the nine patients who completed the course–these six were still abstinent one year after completion of treatment. There were three relapses within six months of successful treatment, and five of the patients decided to discontinue treatment before achieving successful reduction. A larger and better designed study by Russell et al.[12] confirmed the effect of aversive shocks, but also revealed, somewhat surprisingly, that the same result was achieved by contingent or noncontingent shocks–thereby helping to reopen the unresolved questions of how and why aversion works, when it does work.

Another aversive technique involves the delivery of blasts of hot, smoky air into the face of smokers while they smoke. After some discouraging early reports, this method has clocked up some recent successes and appears to repay further study. A third form of aversive therapy that can claim a small degree of support is called satiation.[13–14] In this method the smoker is required to smoke rapidly and excessively for prolonged periods. The effect of this is to produce a strong distaste for and even aversion toward cigarettes. The problem here, as with other methods, is in ensuring that the effects are more than transient. We are not yet in possession of sufficient information on which to decide whether any or all of these aversive techniques can be shaped into effective methods for reducing or stopping smoking for satisfactorily long periods. We are, however, in a position to say that they are among the more promising of a host of largely ineffective psychological procedures that have been used, and that they are therefore worthy of further research.

Few of the considerably more elaborate psychological methods have achieved greater success than that achieved by doctors advising their patients that it is in their interest to stop smoking. Reviewing the evidence, Russell points out that in one study, half of all the people who successfully gave up smoking on grounds of health said that they had done so on the direct advice of their doctors. In another study, medical advice given on a single visit produced a substantial and lasting reduction in cigarette consumption in one-third of the sample of patients. In Britain, nearly half of a group of patients visiting a chest clinic stopped smoking for at least three months after being given routine advice, and Williams, working with a similar type of patient, obtained a high rate of cooperation and a remarkably good overall result.[15] No less than 23 percent of the group gave up smoking for the whole of a six-month follow-up period, immediately after a single interview. A further 30 percent gave up smoking for the same duration after receiving additional advice in subsequent interviews.

These are encouraging results, particularly when it is remembered that the advice given was of a fairly simple and routine kind. In none of these studies were elaborate or systematic measures taken. On the other hand, these patients, many of them with chest ailments, had strong reasons for following the advice. It is unlikely that similarly high success rates would be attained by simple, routine advice given to a randomly selected group of patients.

The discouraging results obtained by many of the psychological programs designed to increase self-control led Raw to suggest that greater stress should be placed on comprehensive external controls.[14] In psychological research this distinction between internal and external control has been introduced in analyzing excessive eating, and it may well be that analyzing smoking along these lines would prove profitable. As a minimum, it would be interesting to know if smokers, like excessive eaters, are stimulated by external cues to overindulge themselves – for instance, being offered cigarettes. If it could be shown that many or most smokers are strongly influenced by such external factors, it would follow that modification programs should include attempts to remove or reduce the presence of these cues. Another trend emerging in the research on smoking control is the increasing emphasis placed on the patient's motivation to stop. This movement is strengthened by the fact that almost all forms of intervention, from aversive control to sugar pills, are capable of producing moderate, if short-lived, changes. It is widely believed that one of the main contributors to these nonspecific changes is the intention and desire to stop smoking. Needless to say, the examination and anlysis of these complex concepts will require a great deal of time and effort. It is hopefully anticipated that a better understanding of the motivation to give up smoking will ultimately help us to come to grips with the very great number of people who fail to complete the course in antismoking campaigns or procedures.

It should not be thought that the limited progress made in developing psychological techniques for producing smoking abstinence carries a message of unrelieved pessimism. Some methodological advances have been made,[9] and some obstacles and difficulties have been removed. For example, improved methods of data collection have been developed, a wide range of nonspecific factors in smoking control have been identified, and some important clues to the nature of the motivational factors have been detected.

Minimum effort, maximum effect

Medical practitioners have a powerful weapon in the campaign against smoking but they have not yet chosen to exercise it fully. Given that at present the method that produces the best results is a doctor's advice, and that up to one in three patients will respond positively to a clear medical warning on the subject, "the minimum effort" required is a systematic exploitation of the power of medical practitioners. "The maximum effect" that one can reasonably expect is that up to 30 percent of the smoking population might be persuaded at least to reduce their cigarette consumption by a clear warning administered by a familiar and trusted doctor, preferably during a period of illness. Naturally, the number of people who could be expected in practice to respond satisfactorily to this approach would fall short of 30 percent of the adult smoking population, but even so it might exceed 3 million. This leaves a substantial number of people who will continue to smoke unless other and more successful methods can be developed. As we have seen, so far it is the aversive techniques that show most promise. It is obvious that both the direct method of treating smoking by psychological intervention and the indirect method of persuading and then changing the behavior of medical practitioners need to be gone into with great care. As a priority, it might be best to concentrate on the development of the most persuasive forms of communication for use by medical practitioners.

With regard to methods of direct treatment, the outstanding problems are how to enlist and maintain the cooperation of smokers and how, once abstinence has been achieved, the disappointingly high relapse rate can be cut. In all this, a greater appreciation of the motives that operate in both smokers and in those who are cured is badly needed. We need clarification of the causes of smoking, which, it is to be hoped, will prepare the ground for wide-scale preventive measures.

Obesity

Excessive eating, like smoking and regrettably many other activities, is pleasurable but potentially harmful. From a psychologist's point of view, both habits can be construed as problems of inadequate self-control. Although attempts to increase self-control through psychological means have not met with success in antismoking clinics, modest successes have been achieved in reducing obesity. How can we account for the difference? One possibility was raised by Russell, who argued that smoking is best regarded as a form of drug dependence. There are other differences as well.

Unlike eating, smoking is a superfluous activity; the health risks associated with smoking are the result of indulgence, whereas those associated with obesity arise from overindulgence. In attempting to control smoking one aims for abstinence, whereas the aim in eating control is to achieve moderation. Another difference is that obesity is caused by a combination of factors – excessive (or unwise) eating and insufficient exercise. Hence, attempts to reduce weight should preferably aim to decrease or change food intake, while increasing physical exercise. Many of the popular methods of dieting do include both elements, and for numbers of people with minor weight problems, self-initiated and self-monitored attempts bring satisfactory results. Obese people, however, experience far greater difficulty. Their own attempts to reduce weight are seldom successful, and medical methods are inadequate. This discouraging state of affairs was summarized by Stunkard, a prominent authority on the subject, who concluded that "most obese persons will not remain in treatment and of those that remain in treatment, most will not lose weight, and of those who do lose weight, most will regain it."[16]

As we shall see, some progress has now been made in the use of psychological methods for reducing weight, but in the case of the truly obese person the weight losses have been of statistical rather than clinical significance. While in no way wishing to discourage further attempts to provide psychological solutions, we must keep in mind the possibility that severe obesity may have a mainly physiological basis and therefore be more amenable to physiological remedies. The uncomfortably close behavioral similarites between obese people and obese rats suffering from induced physiological disturbances have been described and analyzed with admirable clarity by Schachter.[17] He has also been responsible for conducting fascinating research on obese people; his main conclusion is that they are excessively "stimulus-bound." That is, their eating behavior is determined mainly by the sight and availability of food – in contrast to people of average weight, whose eating is determined mainly by internal cues, particularly stomach contractions or distension. Obese people experience hunger in a way that "has almost nothing to do with the state of (their) gut." In a series of experiments Schachter has found that fat people tend to eat whatever tasty food is in sight, even after a meal, whereas other people tend to eat only until they feel full.[18] Although fat people tend to eat fewer meals, they generally eat more, and more quickly. They are, however, less inclined to expend effort in order to eat (e.g., they prefer forks and spoons to chopsticks when eating Chinese food!) and are *less* likely to complain of hunger when there is no food. This last observation, consistent with Schachter's thesis that obese people are stimulus-bound, has been put to good use in designing behavior-modification programs.

Recently, psychologists have begun to pay more attention to the problem of weight reduction, partly as a clinical problem in its own right and partly because it provides a useful analogue for research into psychological techniques for increasing self-control. The aversive conditioning methods that yielded some positive results in controlling smoking have proved to be disappointing when applied to problems of weight control.[2]

Other techniques of behavior modification, with the exceptions to be described presently, have also produced discouraging results. The most promising results have in fact been achieved by systematic application of self-control programs, and Stunkard endorsed them favorably.[16] In a review of progress he said that "these programs have been used to compare behavior modificiation with a variety of alternate treatment methods. Every one of eight such studies has reported results favoring behavior modification, an unusual example of unanimity in this heterogeneous and complex disorder." These studies have characteristically relied on weight changes as the main indicator of success or failure, and although it is true that the studies referred to (and others reported more recently) all report significant reductions in weight, they were not unqualified successes. The amounts of weight lost were not large in absolute terms; few of the programs achieved the goal of producing extensive and lasting losses in weight.

The first comprehensive weight control program was introduced by Ferster in 1962,[19] developed by Stuart,[20, 21] and tested by several other psychologists. The construction of the program has been influenced by the work of Schachter who, as we have seen, argues that obese people are more influenced by external cues than are their thinner fellows.[22] Considerable emphasis is therefore placed on the importance of ensuring that the obese person keeps food in a specific place (e.g., the kitchen) and eats at restricted times. Additionally, special techniques were introduced to help people to eat more slowly, chew smaller portions, pause between mouthfuls, and so on. The purpose of these instructions is to help the subject achieve greater control over the act of eating. In order to encourage and then maintain this new style of eating, the subjects are placed on a points system. Exercise of the suggested procedures during and between meals earns a predetermined number of points, which are then converted into money and donated by the subject to a favorite charity. Administration of the treatment program requires between six and ten visits spread over three to eight weeks, followed by monthly follow-up consultations. Before the self-management program starts, the participants are required to keep detailed records of the size and time of their meals and other circumstances of their eating habits. These data are analyzed and used in the construction of the individual subject's program. It is worth noticing, in passing, that the act of carrying out this self-monitoring activity is usually followed by a clear although modest reduction in eating. (Smokers also reduce consumption when asked to record each cigarette smoked.) The exercises designed to reduce eating habits are supplemented by physical exercises, carried out daily if possible. Successful completion of these exercises is rewarded on the same system of points.

This general approach was used by Penick, Stunkard, and their collaborators in a treatment trial involving thirty-two obese patients.[23] More than half of the patients who participated in the program lost more than twenty pounds, and 13 percent of them lost more than forty pounds. These losses were significantly greater than those achieved by a matched control group of patients treated in the traditional way. The persistence of the improvements as seen at the six-month follow-up time is a particularly encouraging feature of this report, bearing in mind that all too often in the past apparently successful weight-reduction programs have been quickly followed by relapses.

Another common weakness of many forms of treatment for obese patients is the high attrition rate. It is not unusual to find that more people give up the treatment prematurely than stay the course. Until the advent of these new behavioral self-control programs, it was unfortunately the case that therapists found it easier to lose patients than pounds. Although Stunkard's optimistic review of progress is not misplaced, at least three important obstacles need to be overcome before the new methods can be widely recommended. We need to increase the power of the programs so that the amount of weight lost reaches clinically significant levels, take special measures to ensure that relapses are kept to a minimum, and maintain the active cooperation of a far greater proportion of patients.

10   Psychiatric psychology

Most clinical psychologists are still dealing with problems of abnormal behavior. Courses in clinical psychology are mainly psychiatric in content, the journals publish mostly psychiatric articles, and psychologists for the most part practise psychiatric psychology. Indeed, many are still employed in departments of psychiatry. Before the expansion from psychiatry into other branches of the health services alters the style and purpose of clinical psychology, it might be enlightening to examine the results achieved by the collaboration between the two disciplines, thus far, with a view to developments in the new branch, behavioral medicine.

The test era

In the first place, what contributions have psychologists made to the development of psychiatry? Although they include the introduction of some practical measures, to be described presently, we agree with the view that the most useful psychological contribution was "ideological." The postwar influx into clinical psychology of rigorously trained experimental psychologists provided welcome support for those psychiatrists who were advocating the introduction of stricter scientific standards into their subject. There can be little argument that the standards and methodology of psychiatry have improved over the past two decades, despite some lingering desires for a return to the confines of nineteenth-century Vienna. The balance has shifted from excessive speculation towards increasing reliance on empirical findings.

On the practical side, the early clinical psychologists were bogged down by the hard-won success of their intelligence tests. For a few decades their colleagues in psychiatry continued to pepper them with request forms reading "IQ test please." Years of "test bashing" produced a dislike of testing that was only partly mitigated by the distractions of Rorschach ink-blot cards, Thematic Apperception Tests (TAT), Minnesota Multiphasic Personality Inventories, and other finery. The projective tests, such as the Rorschach, with their promise of providing mental X-rays, have not been a success[1,2] but the new generation of psychometric tests do earn their keep. Tests of intelligence, after a period of excessive use, now have a valuable if limited place in educational and psychiatric work.

The story of the Rorschach test, illustrative of the fate of other projective tests as well, is sobering. The test consists of ten cards, each depicting an ink blot. The cards are presented to patients in a fixed sequence, and they are asked to respond freely to the cards and describe their perceptions. Responses are classified and then interpreted, and frequently given weight in reaching psychiatric diagnoses. There are, however, convincing reasons for concluding that the test is neither reliable nor valid. Consider the fate of only one aspect of the frequently complex types of interpretation placed on the subject's account of his perceptions. Great significance was attached to the person's reaction to the last cards, which contain color. Literally hundreds of journal papers were written on the interpretation of reactions to the color on these cards, but recently research has shown that the test results are unchanged when specially produced achromatic cards are substituted for the colored ones. On a broader scale, the important and ambitious study reported by Little and Shneidman in 1959 examined the validity of the conclusions drawn from patients' responses to projective tests.[3] They obtained the services of acknowledged experts in projective test analysis and compared their independently determined interpretations of test protocols obtained from normal people, neurotic, and psychotic patients. They also compared conclusions drawn from the Rorschach test data with those deduced from other sources, including tests.

The findings revealed such extensive and serious disagreements and errors in diagnosis as to bring into question the use of the Rorschach test on any patient, at any time. Despite their brave attempts to draw some comfort from the study, Little and Shneidman concluded that "diagnostic labels based upon blind analyses of protocols may be quite wide of the mark and the present analysis indicates that judges may not even be shooting at the same target" (p. 11). As we shall see, this is an understatement.

The first test participant was *normal*. Like all the others, he completed three projective tests (including the Rorschach) and one other psychological test. His results on each of the four tests were interpreted by four experts, giving a total of sixteen independent diagnoses. These judges turned up no less than ten different pathological labels! He was described variously as suffering from schizophrenia, anxiety neurosis, hysteria, psychopathic personality, brain damage, character neurosis, homosexual tendencies, and possible alcoholism. The next person, also normal, received *twelve* different diagnostic labels out of the sixteen offered. They included conversion hysteria, compulsive neurosis, homosexuality, neurotic depression, anxiety neurosis, character neurosis, schizoid character with depressive trends, and so on. At the other extreme, participant number eleven was suffering from schizophrenia. Although nine of the sixteen diagnoses were correct in this case, he was variously described as being normal, neurotic, immature, and suffering from hysteria. The tenth person, also suffering from schizophrenia, produced even less satisfactory responses from the experts. Three of the four Rorschach judges failed to conclude that he had schizophrenia. Instead he was variously described as having a "compulsive character," an "inadequate character," and an obsessional personality. The fifth person was suffering from a neurotic disorder but was diagnosed by no fewer than eleven of the judges as being psychotic. Research work of the character briefly described here has led many psychologists to the conclusion that projective tests are misleading. In all, projective test interpretations are an unfortunate example of interprofessional collaboration that led to a sorry outcome.

Therapy

It could not be expected that psychologists, rarely with less than five years and often with more than eight years of university study, would be content for long with "test bashing." By the early 1960s they were showing an enthusiastic and active interest in therapy. For many of them, therapy meant psychotherapy, and psychotherapy meant Freudian-based interpretive therapy. Although the evidence on the therapeutic effects of interpretive treatment is unsatisfactory,[4] psychologists are conducting this form of therapy in increasing numbers, to the discomfort of some members of the psychiatric profession, who give the impression that they are in favor of restrictive practices. Meanwhile an alternative approach to treatment and rehabilitation, called behavior modification or behavior therapy, was developed, largely by psychologists. These procedures are now beginning to make an effective contribution. Many of the psychologists who helped to establish the alternative methods were recruits from psychological laboratories, and their approach was distinguished by a concern for experimental controls, measurement, validation, and replicability. An important consequence of this work was the early recognition that what is now referred to as the "medical model" of psychiatric disorders is deficient (see p. 106). Before turning to a consideration of this theoretical advance, it is worth pointing out some of the practical contributions of psychology to psychiatry.

Psychologists introduced some assessment techniques that can help in diagnosis and the evaluation of treatment. These methods range from standardized psychometric procedures such as intelligence tests, aptitude tests, and personality inventories to the less creditable tests of brain damage and the misleading projective tests. They also include the increasingly useful behavioral assessment and observation techniques, improved rating scales, and conceptual tests. An array of psychophysiological measures, which promised sophistication and objectivity, were also developed, but unfortunately they are still beset by serious technical snags.

Psychologists were also responsible for introducing new forms of psychotherapy, perhaps the most notable being the nondirective method of Carl Rogers.[5] He postulated that there are three necessary and sufficient conditions for effective therapy. It was argued that constructive personality change (the suggested purpose of therapy) is facilitated when the therapist is "warm, empathic, and genuine." He added that when these conditions are present in large measure, the resulting improvement will be more striking; however, if any one of these conditions is not present, constructive change will not take place. This approach to psychotherapy has many attractive features, not least of which is the admirable clarity with which Rogers presents his views. They generated a considerable amount of research and, in brief, it has been found that although the three therapeutic conditions described by Rogers may be facilitative, they are not necessary.[4] A particularly challenging aspect of Rogers's theory was his assertion that academic knowledge and training are irrelevant to the practice of effective psychotherapy; any person, irrespective of his training or knowledge, who relates to people in a warm, empathic, and genuine manner can be a successful therapist. Although this issue is far from settled, there are signs that Rogers may be correct.

The practice of nondirective therapy has also drawn attention to the operation of powerful nonspecific factors that make a beneficial contribution to the various types of psychotherapy – and indeed, to the operation of placebo responses (see Chapter 7).

Psychologists made a specific contribution to our understanding of neurosis by helping to identify the occurrence of a high rate of spontaneous improvement among patients with neurotic problems. In a crude early estimate, Professor Eysenck suggested that as many as two-thirds of all neurotic patients improve substantially within a two-year period. Although comprehensive figures are still not available, this estimate is not far off the mark.[5] In addition to the intrinsic importance of the observation that the majority of neurotic patients improve within a comparatively short period, recognition of this high rate of spontaneous improvement cast a new light on claims made by psychotherapists. It was seen that their claims of success rarely exceeded the spontaneous recovery rate, and on occasions fell below it.

Dissatisfaction with the evidence on the effects of various forms of psychotherapy prompted a search for new methods of dealing with behavioral and other problems. One of the most promising of these new departures, behavior modification, consists of a number of techniques, including desensitization, flooding, modeling, aversion therapy, and operant conditioning. The first three are used for the reduction of fear and anxiety states, aversion therapy is used to suppress unwanted behavior, and operant conditioning has a wide range of applications – mostly designed to establish more adaptive behavior. This conditioning method has so far been most successfully applied to the teaching of intellectually handicapped children and adults (see Chapter 2).

Desensitization was developed by Professor Wolpe for the treatment of neurotic disorders in which anxiety is a central element. It has been used extensively in the treatment of neurotic patients, and the procedure and its rationale have been the subject of numerous experimental investigations.[6] The technique involves the gradual and graduated presentation of anxiety-evoking images while the patient is deeply relaxed. The patient acquires the ability to tolerate these fear-evoking images and this improvement usually transfers to the real-life situation. Much of our knowledge about fears and how to reduce them has been obtained from the study of normal people who show an excessive fear of spiders, snakes, worms, and the like. The present state of the experimental and clinical evidence on desensitization can be summarized in this way. Therapy based on desensitization effectively reduces phobic behavior. It is unnecessary to ascertain the origin of a phobia in order to eliminate it, nor is it necessary to change the person's attitudes or to modify his or her personality. The elimination of a phobia is rarely followed by a new problem or symptom. The effects of desensitization are potentiated by "real-life" practice and, where practicable, "real-life" desensitization is preferable to imaginal forms.

A recent off-shoot of the desensitization technique is one in which the patient is exposed to the fear-provoking situation with relatively little preparation. This type of treatment is called flooding, and has achieved some promising early successes in the management of neurotic disorders, especially phobias and obsessional problems. A third procedure that has yielded exceptionally good laboratory results so far is called modeling. This form of treatment derives from the fact that when a fearful person observes someone else acting in a comparatively fearless manner, preferably on many occasions, it will tend to reduce the observer's own fears. In some respect it can be thought of as overcoming fear by imitating a model who can cope relatively boldly in the relevant situation. The therapeutic effect of this type of modeling is greatly enhanced when the person who is afraid follows through the observation of the successful model by copying the model's conduct. This variation is called modeling with participation. The clinical value of modeling has yet to be determined, but it seems probable that it will be put to greatest effect in preventing and overcoming childhood fears.

The clinical effectiveness of the fear-reducing techniques of behavior therapy is attested to by two types of evidence: individual case histories[7] and controlled clinical trials.[8]

Aversion therapy is used predominantly for the treatment of behavior disorders in which the patient's conduct is undesirable but self-rewarding (such as alcoholism and sexual disorders). The treatment is designed to bring about a strong connection between the undesirable behavior and some unpleasant experience (for example, whisky and acute nausea) or to make the unpleasantness a consequence of the undesirable behavior. It is hoped that by repeatedly associating the undesirable behavior with some unpleasantness, such behavior will ultimately cease. Because of the pleasure that most of the disorders usually treated by this form of technique are capable of producing, it is often necessary and desirable to introduce alternative forms of satisfaction for the patient concerned. So, in the case of a person suffering from bizarre sexual fetishism, the aim of treatment would be to suppress the undesirable behavior and encourage more acceptable and satisfying forms of sexual activity. Although aversion therapy is rated by most patients as being less unpleasant than a visit to the dentist, it has aroused a certain amount of controversy. The majority opinion seems to be that as it involves the administration of unpleasant stimulation, no patient should be offered the treatment as a first choice; and it should certainly not be given except with the informed consent of the patient. The clinical effectiveness of aversion therapy has not yet been determined with accuracy, but it seems to be effective in the treatment of certain kinds of sexual disorders and moderately effective in the treatment of alcoholism.[9]

Operant conditioning treatment techniques are derived from the research reported by B. F. Skinner, and their particular strength is that they enable one to generate and shape new kinds of behavior. Roughly speaking, this is achieved by rewarding effective and appropriate behavior and by withholding rewards after inappropriate and ineffective behavior. The constructive power of these procedures has been of great value in the management of behavior problems that arise because a person has for one reason or another failed to acquire appropriate behavior. So, for example, it has had considerable success in helping to train retarded people to care for themselves, feed themselves, avoid soiling and wetting themselves, engaging in more easily understood communication, and so on. It has also been applied with a slight measure of success in the training or retraining of speech-deficient children.

The full clinical value of behavior modification methods is still under assessment: discussions of recent progress can be found in the works of Kazdin and Wilson[8], Marks,[10] Meyer and Chesser,[11] Rachman,[4] and Feldman and Broadhurst,[12] among others. In a recently published special report, *Behavior Therapy and Psychiatry,* the American Psychiatric Association concluded that behavior therapy procedures "now unquestionably have much to offer informed clinicians in the service of modern clinical and social psychiatry." It is now an accepted form of treatment, and the British and American psychiatric associations, among others, consider that it is necessary for psychiatric trainees to receive instruction in the subject.

Taking the long view, an important contribution of the psychologists to psychiatry was their introduction of improved methodology and heightened critical standards. They also made a useful contribution to our understanding of certain types of psychological abnormality, especially those of a neurotic type and most notably phobias and compulsions. However, their major theoretical contribution may prove to be their successful criticisms of the undiscriminating and hence misleading application of the medical model to problems of abnormal behavior.

Psychiatry's contribution

The contributions of psychiatrists to psychology have been of a different kind and can be grouped in three categories: the provision of facilities, introduction to clinical methods and material, and education in patient care. Psychiatry was the first medical speciality to promote psychological work. Positions were created for psychologists, and they received support and encouragement from their psychiatric colleagues who, earlier than other medical personnel, had the prescience to recognize the importance of psychological factors in their work. Many psychiatrists invited their new colleagues to enter the front line of daily practice, and the effect of this was to promote the growth of a socially conscious group of applied scientists skilled in helping people in psychological distress. In this way a bridge was built from the often remote psychological laboratories, furnished with memory drums and small animals, to clinics crowded with unhappy and handicapped people.

The clinical applications of psychology helped to provide a more human aspect to the science. In earlier years students who entered psychology eager to gain an improved understanding of their own and other people's behavior were sometimes bewildered and disappointed by the discovery that psychological texts devoted most of their space to extensive descriptions of rodent behavior, lightened by references to trivialities of human behavior. In this setting, the challenge offered by psychiatrists of grappling with the intellectual and practical problems of abnormal human behavior was welcome and refreshing.

Although psychiatry and psychiatrists benefited by the arrival of clinical psychologists, there was a price to be paid. They sometimes had to suffer psychologists who affected a superior scientific understanding and even a superior morality. The phenomenal growth of clinical psychology led to a situation in which psychiatry often lost in the competition for funds. Interprofessional disagreements arose in delineating the borders between the two professions, particularly in the practice of psychotherapy, and American psychiatrists fought a losing and needless battle to obtain the exclusive right to therapeutic services. Elsewhere, as in many parts of Europe, the battle has not yet been joined. Although the demand for psychiatric services so far exceeds the supply that no psychiatrist is in danger of applying for welfare, psychiatrists feel understandably pressed by the rapid multiplication of psychologists. To make matters worse, the psychologists are rarely grateful, and indeed are too often resentful.

The collaboration with psychiatry also gives rise to some difficulties for psychologists. Even when their skill, training, and experience are superior to those of their colleagues in psychiatry, psychologists are almost always subordinate. They may find themselves being patronized. Final "clinical responsibility" (rarely defined) almost always rests with the psychiatrist, senior or junior. So, for example, psychiatric residents in their first year of training are in a position to interfere with the work of the most experienced of clinical psychologists, who might have as many as thirty years' or more experience. Again, the status and salary of a psychiatrist are almost always higher than those of a counterpart in psychology. The difference was explained by a psychologist: "What is the difference between a psychiatrist and a psychologist? Thirty thousand dollars a year."

On the scientific side, the medical approach of psychiatrists sometimes has the effect of inhibiting or distorting psychological thinking and practice. The excessive use of intelligence tests, for example, was partly the result of pressures from psychiatrists for this type of reassurance. A vast amount of psychologists' time was wasted – time that could have been devoted to research and to the care and comfort of distressed people. More important, however, was the way in which psychologists, exposed to the medical model of abnormal behavior, accepted it uncritically for over thirty years. This unfortunate influence was an obstacle to scientific advance.

A last example of the undesirable effects of an overzealous use of the medical approach can be seen in respect of homosexuality. In less than twenty-five years it has undergone three major transformations. First it was a crime, then it became a psychiatric symptom, and now it is being seen as an acceptable expression of sexual diversity, no longer abnormal.

What is the medical model?

It is no easy task to explain the weaknesses of the medical model because there is no single agreed version of what the model looks like. In our view, the medical model of abnormal behavior includes some combination of the following features. First and foremost, it is assumed that most forms of abnormal behavior fall within the scope of medical knowledge and practice. Psychological problems or problems of abnormal behavior are regarded as being analogous to physical abnormalities. Many types of abnormal behavior from hallucinations to truancy, from stuttering to repeated drunkenness, and from extreme shyness to premature ejaculation, are considered to be manifestations, that is, symptoms, of illness. Hallucinations are frequently interpreted as a symptom of psychotic illness (insanity), excessive shyness often is taken as an indication of neurotic illness, and so on.

The illnesses inferred from the occurrence of abnormal behavior, regarded as symptoms, are generally construed as having an inner cause. The cause is often assumed to be physical in nature – specifically, an infection, injury, or systemic dysfunction. Although the psychoanalytic theory of mental illnesses is more complex, it shares the major assumption of an inner etiology that gives rise to symptoms. In place of physical causes of illness, Freud made the important substitution of complex psychological causes (for instance, an unresolved Oedipus complex), but he continued to theorize within a medical model.

The state of illness denoted by abnormal behavior is regarded as being different from and discontinuous with a healthy state (characterized by normal behavior). In illness, it is assumed that either one's judgment or control, if not both, are impaired. The illness is assumed to have a distinct etiology and to run a determined course; it has a prognosis.

The appearance of symptoms, in mental illness the appearance of abnormal behavior, requires classification and diagnosis. The main diagnostic groups are neurosis, psychosis, and personality disorder. Once a diagnosis is made, forms of treatment and care are advised or administered (by doctors, in hospitals or clinics). There is an emphasis on physical forms of treatment and, as in physical illnesses, this often comes down to the prescription of drugs.

It is assumed that the process from diagnosis to treatment and aftercare should be controlled and largely conducted by medical personnel. Hence, to return to our earlier examples, excessive shyness or premature ejaculation or stuttering are seen as medical problems – requiring diagnosis and treatment. Another important aspect of the medical model is the assumption that a mental illness, having an underlying cause, is best dealt with by treating this *underlying* cause. Tackling the symptoms, that is, the abnormal behavior itself, is at best superficial. Even when the abnormal behavior is successfully modified, the substitution of another manifestation of the underlying cause can be expected – a substitute symptom in fact. The medical model virtually precludes attempts to modify abnormal behavior in a direct manner.

For a long while the medical view of abnormal behavior as illness went unchallenged, partly no doubt because it is an appropriate model for some types of disorder. Some of them fit comfortably into a medical schema. For example, paresis is a syphilitic infection that damages the brain and results in abnormal behavior, including delusions, impaired memory, and so on. Similarly, Korsakoff's syndrome, a disorder resulting from prolonged abuse of alcohol, is characterized by abnormal experiences, confusion, impaired memory, and sensory disturbances.

Psychologists followed their psychiatric colleagues in overgeneralizing from examples such as paresis to a wide variety of disorders in which abnormal behavior or experiences are an important feature. Thus a person with excessive fears was considered to be neurotically ill, a man who stole repetitively was said to suffer from a psychopathic illness, a woman who was persistently unhappy was diagnosed as having a depressive illness, a man who could not maintain friendships was suffering from interpersonal problems indicative of a personality disorder. The view that abnormal behavior is a medical problem gained such wide acceptance that nowadays psychiatrists accept patients complaining of such diverse problems as homosexuality, excessive drinking, impotence, marital unhappiness, reading retardation, delusions, stuttering, occupational inadequacy, bed wetting, compulsive handwashing, delayed speech, inability to use public transport, exhibitionism, social isolation, and many others.

Without laboring the point by examining each of these examples in turn, it is apparent that many of them (for instance, fear of transport, marital difficulties, occupational inadequacy) are unlikely to be the symptoms of an illness in the senses described earlier. There is no clear division between these problems and others of ordinary living; there is little cause for assuming an underlying pathology. And, of course, it is rare to find a physical basis for problems of this kind, or a single cause or an inner cause. Almost always, an analysis of the problem reveals several contributing factors, present and past. One is obliged to consider the person's earlier experiences, present social and occupational circumstances, recent stressful events, and other factors, and then use them to build up an explanation that attaches different emphases to the many variables involved and to the way in which they have combined to produce the behavior that is constituting a problem. One assembles a psychological model incorporating many factors.

Searches for an underlying cause, physical or mental, and an exclusive reliance on physical methods of treatment are seldom successful. If bed-wetting, compulsive handwashing, stuttering, exhibitionism, excessive drinking, and many other examples are approached as illnesses, then productive and sensible formulations might be precluded. It is not clear why these problems should be regarded as falling within the province of medicine, and there is less cause for considering them to be psychiatric problems. Indeed, even if they were illnesses or signs of illness, there is little in the syllabus of medical colleges to prepare a practitioner who is called upon to analyse or modify them. Courses in psychology, particularly those dealing with abnormal behavior, would be more pertinent. In recognition of this point of view, medical schools are now placing greater emphasis on psychological and other behavioral sciences, and we are seeing the growth of behavioral medicine as a branch in its own right.

Returning to the major argument, many psychologists and increasing numbers of psychiatrists now feel that the medical view of abnormal behavior and experiences was unduly stretched from those instances where it is appropriate, to cover an impossibly large and diverse group of problems. Apart from the psychotic disorders (mainly schizophrenia), autism, paresis, and those disorders caused by injury, growths, or infections, there are not many contemporary psychiatric problems that qualify unquestionably for the label of "illness."

We should also point out that it is no longer unanimously agreed that schizophrenia is a form of mental illness. There are critics who prefer to regard the constellation of abnormal behavior and experiences called schizophrenia as being unusual but not pathological. Certainly it still is not possible to demonstrate either that the cause of schizophrenia is physical, or that there is any one underlying cause. It is also known that the diagnosis of schizophrenia is more widely used in the United States than in Europe; certain American types of schizophrenia would not be so diagnosed in Britain.[13] These two points are common targets of the critics who also remark on the acknowledged fact that the families of schizophrenic patients are on average more disturbed than other families. Despite these problems there are reasons for retaining the view that schizophrenia, at least in the strictly defined sense, is a form of illness.[14] There is strong evidence of a major genetic contribution to schizophrenia, it does follow expected courses, it has a typical age of onset, and it does carry a reasonably clear prognosis. The affected person's judgment and control commonly are impaired, and his or her behavior is usually discontinuous with normal forms in some important respects.

Even more difficult problems of distinction arise in consideration of persistent unhappiness. When does it qualify for the clinical label of "depression"? And is depression an abnormal experience, or an illness, or both? In practice, the clinical label is generally applied to people who suffer from intense and prolonged unhappiness. The dividing line is rough and hence awkward to use, especially in borderline cases. However, there is a plausible case for subdividing depression into two main types. If further research produces the hoped-for biological (probably biochemical) distinction between the two postulated types of depression, it will help to clarify the debate about whether and when persistent, severe unhappiness can reasonably be considered to be a form of illness. It is also worth recalling that until relatively recent times, persistent unhappiness was *not* considered to be a form of illness; instead, such people were described as being melancholic.

Seligman's[15] ambitious theory of depression, based on the concept of learned helplessness, is an excellent example of an alternative *psychological* account of depression and has provoked a great deal of research and thinking. There is a clear contrast between the stimulating freshness of this psychological theory and the stagnation of the traditional clinical approach to depression. Essentially Seligman argues that most depressions are manifestations of a sense of helplessness that arises when we feel unable to reduce the likelihood of a highly aversive event, or feel unable to increase the likelihood of a greatly desired outcome. It seems to the person concerned that there is little or no connection between his or her acts and their outcomes – where and when it matters. The status of the theory has been the subject of extensive analyses and discussion (see especially the revision by Abramson, Seligman, and Teasdale[16]), but the details are outside our present concern. For our purposes it serves as an encouraging illustration of the vitality of a psychological analysis of behavioral and emotional problems. *All that is required is one last step toward a fully independent psychological analysis.* Instead of trying to tailor the theory to match the medical diagnostic category of depression, Seligman and his colleagues could study human helplessness in its own right, and not merely in the hope of demonstrating a medical analogue. Instead of taking psychiatric diagnoses as our boundary stone, we should look toward the work of Kafka and others. The interest and potential value of gaining an improved understanding of the important conse-quences and causes of human helplessness transcend the current clinical concept of depression. This concept (excluding endogenous, biological forms) is marred by overinclusiveness, a lack of specificity, and the absence of a plausible supporting theory. By concentrating instead on the nature, genesis, and consequences of a sense of helplessness – ap-proached as an important psychological phenomenon in its own right – psychologists are far more likely to add to our understanding of the sense of futility, apathy, and related dysphoric phenomena. In turn, an advance of this kind is more likely than clinical studies to lead to practical new psychological methods of helping people to deal with dysphoria in its various forms. The clinical concept of depression can be bypassed on the way to a wider and more profound view of human helplessness, and of hopelessness.

The differences between mental illness and behavioral problems are not always straightforward. There are instances where "mental illness" is indubitably the correct way to construe the problem, and other examples where the term "illness" is inappropriate. It is necessary to find a clear path between these two extreme points of view by careful analysis of each example.

The most promising basis for distinctions probably is that of dysfunc-tion instead of damage, but we are immediately confronted with the intricate and difficult problems of defining psychiatric dysfunction.

Is the distinction between "illness" behavior and other types of ab-normal behavior a mere quibble? In view of the practical and scientific implications of such a distinction, we feel that, despite the complexities involved, it is more than verbal exercise. The label given to a person with psychological difficulties can of course have a significant effect on the way in which he views himself. When we describe a person's difficul-ties as being a manifestation of illness, it is usually assumed that his responsibility for his own conduct is impaired; the problems are regarded as being largely beyond his control. This approach encourages passivity. "If I am ill," the argument goes, "then cure me." And we might add, in passing, that cures are usually expected to arrive in the shape of pills. Many of the people who reject the medical model of psychological prob-lems have significantly substituted the word "client" in place of "pa-tient."

If we approach a person's psychological difficulties as problems of behavior and experience, avoiding any suggestion of illness, he is more likely to retain a feeling of responsibility and to participate actively in the development of satisfactory alternatives. An exhibitionist who is given a medical diagnosis, informing him that he is ill, may be less willing to cooperate actively in carrying out a program designed to stimulate satisfactory sexual alternatives and improved self-control. He believes that publicly displaying his genitals is the symptom of an illness and hence is more likely to ask for pills, or even for an operation.

If one develops the argument that many of the personal difficulties currently regarded as signs of illness are in fact better seen as problems of behavior, it becomes necessary to consider *where* and *by whom* assistance should be arranged. As the people in difficulty are not patients in the ordinary sense and are not in need of *treatment*, it might be preferable for them to attend advisory or guidance agents of some description. As a matter of fact, this is the course taken by most people. Reviewing a number of surveys and other investigations, Bergin pointed out that "the majority of people who experience psychological disturbance do *not* seek out mental health professionals for treatment. Many of them seek counsel, advice, and support from a variety of helping persons, including friends, teachers, clergymen, and lawyers."[17] In one of the surveys, it was also found that respondents expressed greater satisfaction with the help they had received from people other than psychiatrists or psychologists. This finding calls to mind the startling observation made by Professor Jerome Frank in 1968, that in the United States more people are treated by religious healers and chiropractors than by psychiatrists and psychologists combined.[18] If our argument has merit, then plans and actions based on the distinction between illness and personal problems will be more rational and more effective than contemporary psychiatric or psychological services – and perhaps also more effective than religious healing, based as it is on an illness model of a different type. Prayers and prescriptions would be replaced by behavioral analyses, counseling, relearning, and environmental modifications.

At a psychological center the person in difficulty would consult specialists in behavior, people who have been trained in psychology and behavior modification, with or without a background of medical training. Naturally, people suffering from mental illness would remain in the care of psychiatrists; medical personnel interested in behavioral problems could readily acquire the necessary skills and, as mentioned earlier, medical schools are now devoting much more attention to psychological topics. Medical students of the future can be expected to spend less time studying Henry Gray on anatomy and more time reading Jeffrey Gray on fear.

Attempts to provide guidance of the type we are advocating should be preceded by an analysis of the abnormal behavior or experiences, or both, and the findings then used in designing a program of behavior modification. The aim of these programs is not the achievement of a "cure"; instead they are intended to help the person to develop more adaptive behavior and to reduce unadaptive and distressing behavior or experiences. In many instances there is no need to construe the problem in terms of illness; it would be misleading to speak of "treatment" and impossible to "cure" anything.

Psychological problems need psychological solutions. If it appears that an overprotected young man's compulsive handwashing arose out of a steadily growing fear of germs and that the fear was being maintained by the temporary relief obtained from handwashing and by excessive parental concern, several steps might be considered. The parental behavior and attitudes might be modified by direct guidance and example. The man's fear of germs might be reduced by desensitizing him. Attempts could also be made to encourage increasingly independent behavior, including perhaps a move from home.

In this example, easily multiplied, little is gained by calling the man ill (which he probably is not), and no single or physical underlying cause is assumed. The problem behavior is analyzed, several putative contributing factors are identified, and a program of modification is designed. It can be seen that a medical approach to this example of abnormal compulsive behavior is not the only model available.[19] When it assumes a false identity between compulsive problems and the illnesses typified by problems such as paresis, the medical view can be misleading. If it were strictly adhered to, it would rule out attempts to deal with the problem behavior directly. In the present example, direct attempts to reduce the frequency and duration of handwashing would be inadvisable. For a considerable time, in fact, people suffering from this type of difficulty were advised, as were their relatives, to avoid restricting the excessive washing. The elimination of the symptom of handwashing, it was argued, was certain to be followed by the appearance of a new and possibly more serious symptom or illness. Despite this view and the advice given, attempts were made at direct modification of excessive handwashing. Research has shown that even when direct modification is successful new symptoms or difficulties rarely arise.[8,10,19,20]

Sanity and insanity

The distinction between the mental illness model and the psychological approach is also of considerable professional significance. Problems that are manifestations of mental illness should, without argument, remain the responsibility primarily of psychiatrists; naturally, other types of personal problems need not fall within the competence of psychiatrists. In 1973, a Working Party of the Royal College of Psychiatrists in Britain submitted a Memorandum to the Department of Health expressing their views on the role of the psychological services in the Health Service.[21] Despite the inflexibly conservative opinions stated in that Memorandum, the Council of the Royal College accepted it. Although numbers of British psychiatrists have since expressed their strong disagreement with this document of the Royal College, at the time of writing it remains the official view of the profession. The Memorandum rejects all criticisms of the mental illness model:

It is recognized that there is a school of thought which denies the concept of mental illness and considers that the symptoms hitherto classified as mental illness, mental disorder, neurosis, psychosis, personality disorder etc., should be regarded as psychological behavioural maladjustments and should be treated outside the medical ambit. These views are not acceptable to the College.

Among a host of weaknesses that will ensure its early relegation to the archives, the Memorandum tacitly assumes that the recognition of mental illness is a straightforward matter. In fact, contemporary diagnostic systems are blunt and faulty – and the source of considerable difficulty in applying the medical model. The existence of reliable and valid diagnostic systems would of course enhance the value of a (circumscribed) medical model. As Kendell and others have shown, there are serious diagnostic disagreements, particularly between British and American psychiatrists.[13] A disturbing report by David Rosenhan, a noted psychologist at Stanford University, provides dramatic evidence of serious failures of current diagnostic practice.[22] He set out to discover if sane people could be distinguished from insane people.

Eight sane people, including five mature professional workers, gained admission to a total of twelve different psychiatric hospitals[3] by complaining that they were hearing voices. The quality of the hospitals ranged from poor to excellent, from inadequately to well staffed. The eight pseudopatients made no alteration in their appearance, accounts of their personal histories, or present circumstances except for those details that might have revealed their true identity. On admission to the ward, all the pseudo-patients stopped acting as if they were hearing voices; they behaved normally from the time of admission until discharge. Each person had to obtain his or her discharge entirely on personal initiative, and this took an average of three weeks! A charitable interpretation is that this is evidence of a commendable caution, designed to avoid a premature return to ordinary life.

None of the pseudo-patients was detected on any of the twelve admissions. In all but one instance, schizophrenia was diagnosed. No changes were made in any of the twelve diagnoses at any stage – the label sticks. These and related observations illustrate what Rosenhan calls the "tendency to call the healthy sick". It is a common tendency and was operating clearly in the study of Rorschach test interpretations discussed earlier. There, it will be recalled, the responses of normal subjects were classified by twelve of sixteen expert judges as being psychiatrically pathological. And, as we have seen, the eight pseudo-patients in Rosenhan's investigation received during their twelve hospital admissions a total of more than 2,000 pills of various types.

One of the several important conclusions from Rosenhan's study is best expressed in his own moderate terms: "Psychological suffering exists. But normality and abnormality, sanity and insanity and the diagnoses that flow from them may be less substantive than many believe them to be". One can query the general applicability of his findings. Certainly, variations in diagnostic success will be found – some hospitals will do better and some worse. The theoretical challenge of the findings is, however, more significant. Does it mean that we need merely to work toward more accurate diagnostic procedures? Or should we abandon the attempt altogether? In our view the major problem is to be found in the unwarranted extension of medical diagnostic habits and assumptions to abnormalities of behavior, including the mistaken inclusion of behavioral problems under the umbrella of mental illness. The difficulties involved in constructing a workable descriptive system for behavioral abnormalities are so considerable that a continuation of the confusion with illness categories almost rules out the possibility of any progress. Incidentally, it is reasonable to presume that given wider acceptance of and sensitivity to the proposed distinctions between mental illness and behavioral abnormalities, a replication of Rosenhan's study would produce less disturbing results.

Care and cure

It has been observed that we place greater emphasis on cure than on care. More time, effort, and attention are devoted to patients with circumscribed, remediable illnesses than to those suffering from chronic problems or handicaps. People suffering from chronic problems, especially those handicapped by severe intellectual retardation, have traditionally been near the bottom of all lists of priority. The undue emphasis on cures is evident also in psychiatric practices and has been absorbed by psychologists. Recognition of the distinction between behavioral problems and mental illnesses might have the useful result of redistributing medical, psychological, and social efforts, thereby improving the balance between cure and care. It may also assist in replacing the idea that there are only two possibilities – treatment or no help. This view is illustrated by the phrase: "Sorry, there is no treatment for your problem; we can't help you."

As clinical psychologists expand their interests to include other branches of medicine and health services, what course will psychiatric psychology take? The process of expansion is likely to be slow so the majority of clinical psychologists will continue to concern themselves with abnormalities of behavior for a considerable time to come. There will be no shortage of work. The provision of services for people with psychological difficulties or mental illnesses, or both, will require many hands. Fruitful collaboration between psychology and psychiatry will certainly continue. Regrettably, interdisciplinary bickering will also continue. On the scientific side, it is reasonable to anticipate improved understanding of abnormal experiences, the adoption of more satisfactory models of abnormal behavior and of mental illness, improved techniques of assessment, and we can expect advances in the power and applicability of behavior modification procedures. Psychotherapy (of various types) will be practised for some time to come, irrespective of its scientific standing. We can, however, look forward to a more realistic appraisal of its uses and limitations. Even if psychotherapy fails to alter problem behavior, people are likely to offer and receive it – because many unhappy people find that talking to a sympathetic listener is comforting.

11 The psychological impact of hospitalization

Hospital staff are predominantly concerned with the physical state of the people admitted to their care. For inexplicable reasons, the psychological impact of an admission to a hospital, and indeed of the illness itself, has not been a subject of interest or concern until recently. For many people, however, admission to a hospital is an event of considerable emotional significance. From unsystematic observations it seems that at least five manifestations of distress are commonly encountered: fear, increased irritability, loss of interest in the outside world, unhappiness, and preoccupation with one's bodily processes. It is also likely that admission into a hospital, like many other stressful events, produces a sharp increase in our need for social reassurance, particularly from relatives and the professional personnel responsible for our care.[1] Despite these pointers, we have acquired scant knowledge about such matters, and undoubtedly there is a need for psychologists to clarify the nature of the psychological reactions that people have in the hospital, to predict vulnerability and to develop methods for preventing or reducing distress.

We also have some information, although still not nearly enough, about the value of preparation for hospital admission. Janis has suggested that the intensity of fear evoked by a stressful event "can be reduced by prior exposure to a preparatory communication that predicts the event" (p. 94).[1] The idea was tested by conducting extensive interviews on twenty-three patients about to undergo major surgery that was both dangerous and painful. The information obtained in the interviews was supplemented by nursing notes, physicians' reports, and hospital records.

Before the operation three patterns of emotional response were noted. Some patients had high anticipatory fear and displayed emotional outbursts, some expressed concern about the operation but manifested little emotional disturbance, while a third group showed optimism and a lack of concern. It was found that patients who had high *anticipatory* fear displayed considerable anxiety and disturbance after the completion of the operation as well. Somewhat surprisingly, the patients who showed low anticipatory fear displayed a great deal of anger and resentment after the operation and complained a great deal about pain, discomfort, and neglect. The patients who showed a moderate amount of anticipatory fear had the best postoperative morale and were most cooperative. A careful comparison of the patients in the moderate- and low-anxiety

116

groups showed that the only difference was the amount of information they had received before the operation. Patients in the least fearful group had little idea of what to expect, whereas those in the group expressing moderate preoperative fear had been better informed and had more realistic expectations.

This interesting finding was subsequently confirmed by Janis in a study of a further seventy-seven surgical patients. Two-thirds of them had received information before the operation about the unpleasant experiences in store for them and expressed a moderate amount of fear. The remaining third had scanty information beforehand, and showed little preparatory anxiety about the operation. Once again, the patients who had been well informed and expressed moderate anticipatory fear had a more comfortable and less emotional period of convalescence.

Janis' observations have been confirmed in some studies but not in others,[2,3] but the value of preparation, as such, is not in doubt. Research work of a more general kind reported by Richard Lazarus[4] and his colleagues at the University of California supports the idea that realistic anticipation of stress helps to inoculate one. Over a period of many years they have been investigating the effects of stress and possible means of reducing the emotional disruption produced by events of this kind. Broadly speaking, they have found that various forms of rehearsal, including mental rehearsal, serve to reduce the disturbance caused by the stressful events. It seems that rehearsals achieve their effects by reducing at least two of the major determinants of fear and anxiety – novelty and suddenness.[5]

Lazarus emphasizes the importance of having a strategy for coping with stress, and clearly, appropriate rehearsals will stimulate the successful search for adequate means of coping with the real stress when it does occur.[4] Viewed against the background of this type of research on stress and its psychological effects, the potential value of psychological preparation for hospital admissions, surgery, and other painful and uncomfortable treatments is assured.

The experiment carried out by Egbert and his colleagues on ninety-seven adult surgical patients provides some practical encouragement for this approach.[6] The patients were admitted to hospital for abdominal operations and assigned at random to one of two groups, which were, of course, equated on all important factors. Before the operation, the patients in the first group had a visit from one of the surgical team, who gave them information about the operation and its effects. They were told how long the operation would last, where and when they would regain consciousness, the location and intensity of the expected postoperative pain, assurances about analgesic medication, and so on. The patients in the second group did not receive any of the preparatory information.

In the five days after the operation, patients in the first group required only half as much sedation as did the patients in the group who had received no special preparations. The informed group also needed considerably less morphine. As might be expected from the research mentioned earlier, the poorly informed patients experienced more emotional disturbance in the postoperative period. A particularly interesting finding is that although the medical and surgical teams were unaware of the group identity of any of the patients, those who had received preparatory information showed quicker improvement, as a group, than did the poorly informed patients. On average, the informed patients were discharged three days earlier than the others. These interesting findings make it plain that we need a great deal more information about the psychological effects of hospital admissions, treatment, surgery, and the like.

A useful start has been made in testing the strongly held common belief that psychological factors play a major role in recovering from illnesses and surgery. The research by Janis, Egbert, and several other workers has helped to initiate a serious examination of this fascinating question (e.g., Greer et al.[7] related personality factors to recovery from surgery for removing breast cancer, and Melamed[3] tested the value of psychological preparation in aiding recovery from surgery in a group of children). A concerted effort by psychologists and their health-care colleagues to elucidate the psychological determinants of recovery from illnesses is required; the practical and theoretical incentives are extremely inviting.

In our opinion, patients will benefit considerably from determined and systematic attempts to provide psychological preparation for their admission to a hospital and treatment.[8,9] This should include, at least, full factual information, emotional reassurance and some inoculation. We look forward to the day when greater medical and nursing attention is given to the patient's need for emotional comfort and reassurance and less attention to the vagaries of his or her bowel movements.

Children

In 1959 the Platt Committee produced its report on the welfare of children in hospitals. Three of the most important recommendations were that children's hospitals should encourage unrestricted visits by parents, establish mother-and-child units, and admit children only when it is inescapable. These recommendations rest on several psychological assumptions, and we shall draw attention to only two of the most crucial of them. It is presumed that children will find hospitalization to be, at least, distressing; it is further assumed that the presence of the child's parents, particularly the principal caretaker, will help to alleviate the distress. As we hope to show in the course of this chapter, there are grounds for believing that these assumptions are soundly based. There are, however, some disquieting signs that, despite this evidence, the recommendations of the Platt Committee are not being carried out. We shall also consider some psychological techniques that can be introduced into the preparation for, and care of, children in hospitals.

Davie, Butler, and Goldstein found in a longitudinal survey that by the age of seven, 45 percent of the children of a British national sample had been admitted to hospitals at least once.[10] The most common operation requiring hospital admission was removal of the tonsils. One-third of all hospital admissions were considered necessary for this reason. Evidently, admission to hospital at this early age is extremely common and, given that most families have at least two children, there will be few families who have not been affected. It is beyond our competence, as it is beyond our brief, to consider the third of the important recommendations made by the Platt Committee, that is, that children should not be hospitalized if there is a reasonable alternative. For the most part this is of course a medical decision, but it is worth noting that the operation for which most children are admitted, tonsillectomy, is believed by some medical authorities to be carried out too frequently. An editorial in the *Lancet* drew attention to the fact that the benefits of surgical removal of the tonsils and adenoids are often minor or temporary, sometimes both. "The value of tonsillectomy is still controversial."[11] There is some evidence that when the health of children for whom the operation was recommended but *not* carried out is compared to the health of the children who have had the operation, there are few significant differences either shortly after the completion of the operation or some years later. For example, in a report from Birmingham Children's Hospital it was shown that more than half of the 291 children on the waiting list for the operation experienced spontaneous improvements within a two-year period.[12] Leaving medical questions of this type to one side, however, we turn to the psychological effects on the child of being admitted to a hospital.

Unless psychologists or any other group of scientific workers can produce facts or arguments to the contrary, the Platt recommendations are worth implementing on humane and compassionate grounds alone. However, it remains a curious fact of psychological history that part of the impetus for the recommendations came from writings of psychiatrists and psychologists who unwittingly exaggerated the adverse effects that might be expected to accrue from hospital admissions. Many of the writers, including Spitz and Bowlby among others, spoke of the tragic effects that might be expected to arise if children are separated from their mothers. It was implied and sometimes explicitly stated that such a separation, even if temporary, was likely to produce irreversible and serious damage to their personalities, frequently culminating in prolonged antisocial behavior. These alarmist views have been placed in proper perspective in recent years, [11-13] but the recommendations they prompted were humane and sometimes effective. The unfortunate consequence, however, was that many parents and doctors became excessively reluctant to admit children to hospitals and felt needlessly guilty if they did so.

In examining the effects of hospitalization, it is useful to separate the immediate and short-term consequences from the long-term effects that might be expected, say, several months after discharge. Although this elementary distinction is of some value, unfortunately it does not overcome some of the other confounding problems encountered in work of this kind. For example, how can we distinguish between the distress caused by hospital admission and that caused by the illness itself; between the effects of the illness and the medical procedures such as injections, drips, operations, and the rest; or between the effects of admission to a hospital from the distress that might be caused by a separation from the child's parents? Despite the considerable methodological problems, enough information has now been collected to permit some tentative conclusions.

The undesirable effects of prolonged separation, exemplified by long-term institutional care, were sometimes quoted as an argument against hospitalization. An accumulation of information on the effects of short hospital stays (which is of course easier to obtain than data on institutional effects) has now led to a more balanced view.

It appears that the unfamiliarity of the hospital, the staff, and the routine is a major cause of psychological upset. After the initial period of disturbance, most children grow accustomed to the change, and their distress decreases within a few days. Very few show any lasting signs of distress after they have returned home. Children between the ages of seven months and four years are the ones most likely to suffer substantial distress – a finding compatible with other evidence that this is a period during which children are particularly likely to be upset by separation. [13] It appears that well-adjusted children with satisfactory parental relationships cope well with the stresses of hospitalization. Adverse reactions of a long-term character are rarely encountered in children of this type. Preparation for admission can reduce the expected disturbance.

There is evidence of moderate but widespread upset and anxiety in parents when their children are admitted, and some indications that these emotional reactions provoke similar responses in the children themselves. Thus the children of very anxious parents are likely to be more distressed in the hospital.

Evidence of the effects of maternal separation on young children is consistent with these findings and, indeed, the separation of the child from his other mother (and father) may well be responsible for much of the upset experienced on entering the hospital. Yarrow[14] and Rutter[13] have given lucid accounts of the problem of maternal deprivation and placed the matter in its correct perspective. Broadly speaking, temporary breaks in the child's important affectional bonds are seen to produce distress but rarely any long-term consequences — unless the affectional bonds are unsatisfactory before the separation. Long-term disruptions of affectional bonds in young children can, however, have far more serious and enduring adverse consequences. We also need to bear in mind that satisfactory parents, not doctors, nurses, or psychologists, are the most effective people for reducing a child's anxiety, pain, and other forms of distress.

For reasons of this type, and others not mentioned, the Platt Committee recommended that hospital admission should be confined to those cases in which it is unavoidable. Similarly, they recommended the establishment of mother-and-child units, which would of course be of particular value in these cases. By admitting the mother with the child, a double purpose might be served. In the first place, it would avoid disrupting the mother-child bond, and second, the mother would be present and available at precisely that period of the child's life when he or she most needs care, comfort, and affectionate attention. The Committee also recommended that parents should be given unrestricted visiting access to their hospitalized children.

Stacey and her colleagues set out to study the implementation of certain parts of the report in two selected hospitals.[15] They attempted to assess the extent, depth, duration, and individual variations in the disturbance of children admitted to these two hospitals. The main weakness of an otherwise valuable study is the absence of psychological data or expertise. They obtained information about ninety-five children, all under the age of five, who were admitted for tonsillectomy. Two thirds of the children had received some preparation for their admission to the hospital, but of course it was less common among the emergency admissions. They found poor arrangements for the reception of the child and parents. But the most common complaint of the parents was, once again, the inadequacy of the information provided by the hospital staff. One-third of the parents in the sample made this specific complaint, and it was found that nurses were regarded as the least satisfactory source of information. Less than half of the mothers found that the official policy of unrestricted visiting of children under the age of five was actually in operation; one-fifth of the mothers said that they were allowed less than one hour a day with their children.

Stacey and her colleagues relate these deficiencies to the conception that nurses and doctors have of their role.[15] According to Stacey, nurses do not feel that their role "includes playing with or talking to the children on the ward" (p. 110). They felt that their duties were to wash, dress, and serve the children with food. They had almost no contact with the children outside these nursing routines. Although most nurses accepted parents on the ward, almost all of them were opposed to unrestricted visiting. It was found that this attitude was translated into behavior that defeated the official policy of unrestricted visiting. Prolonged or frequent parental visits were plainly discouraged. The message was received; most parents said that they were concerned to avoid "being in the way" – again, "they expect the nurses to be busy . . . and overworked" (p. 115). The nurses had little contact with the parents and were observed to disappear when the parents arrived. There was little provision, physical or social, for parental help, let alone visits. These acts of omission served to discourage parents from visiting.

The authors offer some tentative views on the characteristics of vulnerable children. They suggest that the children who are most likely to experience undue disturbance are uncommunicative, isolated, shy, very young, or only children. Also in this category are children who have recently been separated from their parents or who have overanxious parents.

Stacey and her co-authors end with many sensible suggestions, endorsing the Platt recommendations and adding their own. They urge that occupation should be provided for the children during the day (for instance, by play-group leaders or nursery teachers), as it was found that the majority of children spent an astonishing amount of time entirely on their own during each day. They also recommend the removal of the physical, personal, and professional barriers to parental visits. They would like to see hospital staffs encouraging parents to participate actively in caring for their children, a move that would of course require that space and equipment of a suitable kind is provided (such as feeding chairs, toys, bathrooms, and TV seats). They further recommend improved preparation and health education both at home and in schools and a form of induction process for children about to go into a hospital. All their proposals seem to us to be both desirable and sensible without being overelaborate. They have the great merit of being open to proper psychological, and other, evaluation. To their suggestions we would like to add the following:

1. Attempts to reduce the vulnerability of children by arranging for parental action, school action, and efforts by the local health authorities could be made. For example, it should be possible to show films and videotapes at school of children being prepared for hospitalization and coping with the routines in a hospital. Also, parents could be encouraged to make arrangements for their children to sleep away from home on suitable occasions at a younger age than is perhaps customary.

2. Knowledge about the value of modeling for teaching children how to cope could be exploited in hospitals by using a system of peer models.[16] Each new admission could be assigned to a "veteran" patient who would be asked to guide him through his first hours and through the standard routines required.

3. Direct preparations could be given to children who know that they are to go into the hospital. For example, they could be shown preparatory films, make visits to the ward before admission, practise some of the routines in the hospital setting, and so on.

4. Parents could be told how they can be most effective during the child's period in the hospital. Again, it should be possible to use film and real models in transmitting the knowledge and skill. Parents could be taught how to cope with their own anxieties and how to reduce the anxiety and distress of their children.

5. Nurses and doctors working with children could be taught about the psychology of separations, illnesses, and admissions, and trained to comfort children and encourage the active help of parents. None of these efforts will qualify as successful until the last nurse is heard to explain that she "cannot talk to the children because she has too much work to do."

All these ideas and proposals are unnecessarily elaborate and time consuming – if our health services are for ever to be seen as physically based and oriented. When broader and more compassionate views prevail, the psychological impact of what we do with and for our patients will assume its proper importance.

The value of each of the specific proposals will need to be assessed by appropriate research investigations. There is some evidence, but by no means sufficient in quantity or quality, to support the *general* idea that preparation for the experiences of a hospital admission is of value. In an often quoted study by Prugh and others, the value of psychological preparation for ·admission and the explicit provision of emotional support during the hospital period seemed to be demonstrated in a series of 100 children.[17] These children apparently showed less fear, unhappiness, and emotional upset during their hospital stay than did a comparable 100 children who received neither the psychological preparation nor the emotional support. For a variety of technical reasons, the experimental design used in this study was faulty and consequently the conclusions must be tentative. Unfortunately, the weaknesses in this study, which included a confusing mixture of procedures, the absence of "blind" assessors, and other deficiencies, are also present in the few other studies carried out during this period. A more satisfactory study was reported by a group working at the Yale School of Nursing.[18] In this investigation the children in the experimental group (and their parents) were given information about hospital procedures and a full account of what the child might expect before and after the completion of the operation to remove their tonsils. A comparable group of children in the control condition received normal hospital care, nursing, and medical procedures, but were not given preparatory information or advice. The observations and assessments were carefully controlled, and the major outcome was that the children who received the additional preparation displayed fewer signs of emotional disturbance while in the hospital or during their convalescence at home.

The most reliable and convincing evidence of the value of preparing children for treatment comes from the carefully planned and executed research of Dr. Barbara Melamed,[19,20] working at Case Western Reserve University in Cleveland. So far she has completed five experiments in a systematic program of research into the effects of preparation. The most significant feature of this research is the consistency of her findings – in all of the experiments, psychological preparation was followed by reduced anxiety and more effective and cooperative behavior. The major experiments were conducted on children between the ages of four and twelve admitted to the hospital for elective operations (for the removal of tonsils or repair of hernias), but she has also gathered evidence on the beneficial effects of preparing children for dental treatments.[21]

Overall, the best results were obtained by showing the children a film in which a youngster is shown approaching the hospital, completing the admission formalities, taking a blood test, and talking to the surgeon and anaesthetist. He is then shown waking up in some discomfort after the operation, after which he regains his composure and finally prepares to return home. The film aims to maximize the fear-reducing and instructional value of using a child model, and is narrated by the boy himself. Film preparations are a relatively simple way of providing valuable emotional protection; additional techniques of preparation currently being developed are bound to improve and extend such protection. As Melamed concludes, the psychological preparation of children for medical procedures is a "fertile field" for study.

It is not too early to enquire into the reasons for the beneficial effects of preparation. Our view is that the most satisfactory theoretical framework is provided by the concept of *predictability* and the closely associated concept of controllability. The reviews of the laboratory research on this subject prepared by Seligman[22] and by Mineka and Kihlström[23] are particularly helpful, and their conclusion is that unpredictable (and/or uncontrollable) events can produce "a variety of cognitive, affective, and somatic disturbances" (Mineka and Kihlström, p. 256). The likelihood of an unpredictable event leading to stress effects is increased if the event is significant and potentially aversive (e.g., undergoing an operation). Incidentally, unpredictability has been shown to be unpleasant in its own right. When they are given the choice, people prefer predictable unpleasantness (e.g., a shock) to unpredictable unpleasantness – even when the degree of unpleasantness (e.g., shock intensity) is held constant. Signals that predict a period of safety may be especially important.[22] It is important to know when we can safely relax.

Unsurprisingly, uncontrollable threats are more disturbing and disruptive than controllable threats.[22] Improved predictability, which offers the promise of controllability, is a means of coping with potential or actual stressors.

Thus, predictability is desirable in itself and also increases one's chances of coping with stressors. It follows, therefore, that any psychological procedure that increases a patient's capacity to predict a potentially stressful event or sequence of events is desirable in itself and provides a basis for improved coping behavior. Admission to a hospital, investigatory procedures, surgery, and postoperative events are all potentially distressing events and usually are predictable in part or totally. (Adequate preparation also serves a useful function in telling the patient when he or she is in a *safe* period.) The clinical research into the benefits of psychological preparation that we have described seems to fit well the concepts of predictability and controllability. The subject of preparation offers an unusually clear and promising opportunity for merging practical and theoretical psychology, to the mutual benefit of both branches.

The accumulating evidence[14,24] on the psychological value of preparing adults and children for admissions to and treatment in a hospital is consistent and has the added virtue of being common sense. The sophisticated psychological research on preparing people to cope with various forms of stress is uncommon, but no less sensible for that.

12   Health and stress

An event, or an anticipated event, qualifies for the term *stress* if it is
followed by adverse effects (e.g., stomach ulcers). Because many events
produce adverse effects inconsistently or occasionally or selectively,
they do not always fit the definition of stress. Also, there are marked
individual differences in response to potentially stressful events; one
person's stress is another person's pleasure. For these reasons, the search
for events that have adverse effects on health must take into account
variations in individual reactivity and in circumstances.

As we shall show presently, a stressor, such as a noise, irregularly produces adverse effects and is therefore an occasional or additional stressor.
A single demonstration of the stressful effects of a particular event (e.g.,
an intense noise) is not sufficient to regard it as a consistent or universal
stressor. Comparable events may be stressful in some circumstances, but
beneficial in other circumstances. They may improve one's health. It
should also be remembered that stressful events may produce short-term
or long-term (and therefore less obvious) adverse effects.[1]

Paradoxical reactions

As the belief that certain psychological events are stressful and have an
adverse effect on one's health is so widely accepted, it is as well to begin
by describing some examples in which exposure to seemingly stressful
events had a beneficial effect on health. In his survey of the psychological effects of wartime conditions on British civilians, Lewis[2] found that
the neurosis rate remained steady or even declined. He suggested that
engaging in a socially useful occupation might provide a form of inoculation against stress. Some people who were previously of poor mental
health were said to be considerably improved after taking up some socially necessary work – "they have a definite and satisfying job." Lewis
was able to show that a proportion of chronic neurotics attending outpa-
tient clinics had declined, "since the war has given them interests
previously lacking." Two of our patients provide illustrations of Lewis'
claim. The first patient was a young married woman who was tormented
by obsessional thoughts on the theme of violence. She was partly disabled and had to be admitted to a psychiatric hospital where she re-

mained miserable, distressed, and apathetic. A course of behavioral treatment was instituted, and she began to make slow but clear progress. At this stage her husband, who had previously been in good health, developed an illness that first emerged in an upsetting and dramatic fashion when he had a seizure while they were at a restaurant. The patient dealt with her husband's seizure, and the subsequent medical investigations and difficulties, with assurance and competence. During the course of the two weeks following the onset of her husband's epilepsy, her competent handling of the crisis was accompanied by a discernible improvement in her obsessional problems and mood. The second patient was suffering from a severe and chronic neurosis that was even more disabling than that endured by the first patient. At the time of the "stressful" incident, she too was an inpatient at a psychiatric hospital. She was persistently and pervasively anxious, socially isolated, incapable of working, and almost housebound. At that point, her mother became extremely ill and the patient had to return home to care for her and manage the household. During the few weeks of her mother's serious illness, the patient performed all of the tasks required of her in a satisfactory manner and with little distress or anxiety. For example, she was for the first time in many years able to do all of the household shopping at the local stores and dealt with a number of household problems. During this period she was more energetic, and her mood and general condition improved. In both of these cases, the improvements were observed to occur over a short term, but is is possible that similar events may give rise to long-term benefits. Experiments into the positive effects of exposure to stress are now being attempted.[3]

More facts about stress-produced benefits are needed before attempting to account for the psychological processes involved, but it will come as no surprise if Bandura's theory of self-efficacy, to be discussed later, finds a place in the explanation.

Laboratory stress.

Laboratory investigations of potentially stressful events allow for precise control, but suffer from other limitations. Experiments with human subjects are necessarily confined to acute exposures to potential stressors, and their intensity has to be kept moderately low. At best one can measure the transient effects of potential stressors on psychological performance, psychophysiological indices such as heart rate, and cognitive changes. A rewarding example of this kind of research is lucidly described by Broadbent,[4] who deals primarily with the stressful effects of noise, but comparable studies have been carried out on the effects of excessive heat and of sleeplessness. In many of these experiments, and particularly those on the effects of noise, a major index of the occurrence of adverse effects was based on a vigilance test. In these vigilance tasks the subject has to attend to auditory or visual signals presented at fairly regular rates and interspersed with occasional signals of a special significance. For example, the subject might be required to listen to long lists of digits, paying particular attention to the occurrence of the number seven. Having established their normal performance on a task of this kind, the subjects are then exposed to potentially stressful stimulation. "It is easy to show that the onset of a sudden and unfamiliar noise impairs a very wide variety of tasks. The effect wears off within a matter of minutes, however, and also applies to the sudden ending of a noise which has become familiar. Thus it appears to be a reaction to change of stimulation rather than to prolonged intense stimulation" (p. 401).[4] However once these transient effects have worn off, many tasks are performed "as efficiently in loud noise as in quiet conditions." According to Broadbent, the results are best explained by supposing that noise "produces brief failures in intake and analysis of information." Although noise, or excessive heat, or sleeplessness, are all capable of producing impairments in behavior, the pattern of such impairments differs for the different stressors. Heat gives rise to immediate errors, and sleeplessness slows down reactions without necessarily giving rise to errors. The effects of sleeplessness are most marked during prolonged periods of vigilance or other tasks. In some circumstances these different types of stress combine and interact, but in some interesting examples they appear to act in opposite directions. For instance, the impairments that generally are produced by sleeplessness can be counteracted to some extent by the introduction of noise. Broadbent's interpretation of these and related findings led him to postulate that "low arousal or high arousal produce inefficiency, and performance is best at an intermediate level of arousal. In ordinary terms, a man can be too drowsy for efficient work, or else overexcited and flap" (p. 411). The damaging effects of sleeplessness are most marked when the person is required to carry out tasks that demand rapid actions.

Broadbent concluded from his own experiments and a full review of the literature that the process of filtering information from the environment is particularly sensitive to stress. The efficiency of our filtering processes is impaired under high arousal, and we tend to pay insufficient attention to information from less dominating sources. This leads to errors. In our simplified construction of Broadbent's advanced and complex theorizing, it can be said that under stress the filtering system suffers from an overload of stimulation and impairments follow. Impaired functioning can also result from other processes, but stressful overloads are most likely to be related to health hazards.

Experimental neuroses

The sequence of events leading to breakdowns in function was repeatedly and vividly demonstrated in numerous experiments carried out on animals, starting with the classical experiments carried out in Pavlov's conditioning laboratory more than 50 years ago. If animals are subjected to excessive stimulation, especially under conditions of confinement, they display wide-ranging and persistent disturbances of behavior.[5-8] Their health may be impaired, and disorders ranging from stomach ulcers to cardiovascular dysfunctions have been produced. These breakdowns of behavior and physiological function can be provoked by conflict, frustration, excessive stimulation, or by the presentation of uncontrollable aversive stimuli.

In a convincing series of experiments Weiss[9] showed that animals subjected to unpredictable and/or uncontrollable shock are likely to develop stomach ulcers. "The data consistently show that psychological factors can be even more important than a physical stressor in determining the severity of gastric pathology" (p. 267). The main pathogenic factors identified so far are those of uncontrollability and unpredictability. Conversely, increases in either of these factors serve to reduce the consequences of aversive stimulation.

In their skilful review of several decades of research on experimental neuroses, Mineka and Kihlström[10] confirmed the importance of these two factors. The findings represent one of the "most salient examples of gross behavioral and physiological disturbance ever produced by purely behavioral manipulation" (p. 260). There is abundant evidence that exposure to "uncontrollable aversive events can create a variety of profound affective, cognitive and physiological disturbances" (p. 259). Naturally, it is not possible to replicate these laboratory findings on human subjects (particularly in the case of chronic preparations), but at those points where the animal and human experiments of a related character can be matched, the results are mainly consistent.

The relationship between uncontrollability and unpredictability is a close and subtle one, but Weiss[11] managed to tease apart the stressful effects of these two factors. In one of his experiments, the factor of uncontrollability was held constant in order to determine whether predictable or unpredictable shocks produce greatest stress effects, in this particular case, ulceration of the stomach. The results showed that the rats who received unpredictable shock formed many more ulcers than rats receiving predictable shock, or no shock at all. These and related findings have been used by Seligman[12] to conclude that "in general, men and animals prefer predictable to unpredictable events, and this reflects the fact that no safety is available with unpredictable shock, while safety can be predicted by the absence of the signal for predictable shock" (p. 122). Unpredictability and uncontrollability contribute to the level of stress, but on the other hand, increasing predictability and controllability enable one better to cope with threatening events, and hence reduce their stressful consequences. Acquiring actual and perceived control of threatening events is the best way to reduce or prevent the adverse effects of a potentially stressful experience – a theme that Seligman has developed elegantly. The notion of perceived competence also has a central part in Professor Bandura's unifying theory of behavioral change.[13] In essence, he argues that all methods of inducing constructive behavioral change are successful to the extent that they improve the person's "perceived self-efficacy." These improvements in perceived competence can be promoted by verbal persuasion, by successful accomplishments, or by exposure to competent models.

All three of these events may contribute to the benefits that sometimes follow exposure to stress, but it surely is successful accomplishments that are most likely to produce gainful changes. In the clinical examples described earlier, both patients successfully coped with external stresses – conceivably their benefits were the product of these successes. Bandura might claim that the benefits were mediated by an increase in their self-efficacy – the sense of their own competence.

Although there are important differences between the theories of Seligman and Bandura, they come closest to agreement on the proposition that the acquisition of a perceived sense of mastery reduces fear and the effects of potentially stressful experiences.

There is little doubt that the concept of controllability, and the closely related notion of predictability, enable us to integrate seemingly disconnected information, but some problems remain.[14] To take an indirect example of one of these difficulties, in a survey carried out on U.S. combat troops during the World War II, it was found that despite their growing sense of self-confidence in their military ability, 17 percent of the respondents continued to experience intense fear reactions during combat.[15] Although this information on the minority of soldiers who failed to overcome their fears is admittedly indirect, it may be an exception to the expected relationship between perceived competence and adverse reactions. Exceptions of the other kind, where people report little in the way of fear despite the absence of appropriate sense of competence,[14] confirm that the theory of controllability is not entirely sufficient.

We can sum up by noting that three major determinants of reactions to potentially stressful events, have been identified – overload, uncontrollability, and unpredictability. It is possible that in many circumstances these factors are interconnected. Given repeated experiences of the unpleasant and potentially damaging effects of overloads in a threatening situation, it can be assumed that most people will make efforts to prevent or curtail their recurrence. If the threat of an overload arises in a high-risk situation of great personal importance, a sense of perceived control is likely to be as reassuring and calming as uncontrollability is likely to be anxiety provoking and stressful. A busy air-traffic control officer who foresees an emergency is less likely to react adversely if he knows that he can control the incidental occurrence of an intense and irregular noise. If on the contrary, he perceives the build-up of an emergency and feels unable to do anything about the intense and disruptive noise impinging on him, he is likely to get agitated and upset. Moving from this example of an acute stress event, it is easy to see how the adverse consequences of a combination of overload and uncontrollability might, over a prolonged period, give rise to profound and lasting behavioral and physiological disturbances of the kind so vividly described by Gantt,[5] Wolpe,[8] and others.[6,9,10]

Life stresses

Moving from these laboratory analyses of stressful events and their effects to surveys aimed at unraveling the relationships between stress and health in real life involves a change in methodology and a shift from the theoretical to the concrete. The survey approach is exemplified by the research into what are now called "recent life events." Lists of commonly experienced events that are potentially stressful are compiled, rated for stressfulness by various populations, refined, and then rated.[16,17] The items on the modified list are then given different emphases (weights) according to their mean stressfulness ratings, and the responses of each subject about the occurrence of the various events in his/her recent life can be converted into a set of scores that incorporate differences in their significance. Typical examples of this consensual approach are the following items:

Marital separation – weighted score of 65 out of 100
Change to a new school – 20 out of 100
Trouble with boss – 23 out of 100
Major change in financial state – 38 out of 100

All of these examples are drawn from the schedule of recent experience (SRE) constructed by Richard Rahe.[18] The full list consists of 42 life-change events, which are grouped into four categories – family, personal, work, and financial. On the family scale, the two most stressful events, with their weighted scores out of 100 given in parentheses, were the death of a spouse (100), and divorce (73). On the personal scale, the two most stressful events were detention in prison (63), or a major injury or illness (53). Of the items relating to work, being fired was the most stressful, with a score of 47. Retirement from work was of equal significance, with a score of 45. A major change in one's financial state, and a large loan, received weighted scores of 30 or slightly above.

The major aims of this type of research are (1) to identify connections between significant changes in one's circumstances and the onset of particular illnesses, and (2) to predict the onset of illnesses (with the further aim of taking preventive action). Inevitably, the early research on life changes was retrospective in character, but once a reasonably constructed and weighted scale was available, Rahe[17,18] undertook a set of prospective investigations. He concluded from his research, examples of which are provided later, that "recent life changes appear to act as stressors partially accounting for illness onset. Conversely, when subjects' lives are in a relatively steady state of psychosocial adjustment with few ongoing life changes, little or no illness tends to be reported."[19] One of the largest of the retrospective studies concentrated on the life changes and illnesses reported by 2,500 sailors. The expected association between life change units and illness was confirmed, and the association between changes and illness was most marked in the six months prior to the onset of the illness. For purposes of predicting the onset of illness, the significant events that occurred in the previous six months provided the best basis for prediction.

It should be pointed out that retrospective analyses of this character are not satisfactorily conclusive; moreover, the association between life changes and illness is not particularly striking (e.g., in one major study quoted by Rahe,[16] the correlation was only 0.34). However, in a prospective study carried out on a group of physicians, the connections between life-change units and illness was clearer. The majority of doctors who recorded less than 150 life-change units reported having experienced good health during the year under examination. Approximately half of the doctors who scored between 150 and 300 life-change units reported an illness during the same period. Most persuasively, the few doctors who registered more than 300 life-change units during the year recorded illnesses in 70 percent of the cases. The most convincing evidence of a connection between life-change events and the severity of illness was collected in a study of 247 sailors undergoing a difficult and dangerous course of training in underwater demolition work. The training consists of an extremely stressful four-month program. Illness reports

were high during the training, even among those subjects who successfully completed the course. Their illness rate was ten times higher than
that for comparable sailors carrying out normal duties aboard ship.
Among that large proportion of sailors who failed to complete the training successfully, the illness reporting rate "has been seen to rise to fifty
times that for shipboard subjects."[20]

The work reported by Rahe and his colleagues is a useful beginning. It
has shown the necessity of attaching different weights to various life
changes, it has demonstrated that often there is a connection between
life change events and the onset of illness, and has confirmed that acute
episodes of stress are more damaging to health than the common life
changes that comprise most of the items in the scales. However, the lack
of a clear distinction between positive and negative life changes was
unsatisfactory.

The strategy of measuring the frequency of significant life events and
their relation to illness has been extended beyond physical illnesses
(recently reviewed by Rahe[16]) to include psychiatric illnesses. The research carried out by Paykel[21] and his colleagues at Yale University was
conducted with care and a full awareness of the methodological and
conceptual problems involved. They were able to conclude that their
"findings strongly support the role of life events in the onset of clinical
depression. Moreover, they suggest some degree of specificity in that
exits (from interpersonal contact) and undesirable events appear particularly related to depression, while their opposites, entrances and desirable
events, were not implicated."[22] Their first major study was carried out on
185 depressed patients who were compared to control subjects of comparable demographic status drawn from the same urban population as the
patients. Both groups of subjects were intensively investigated in an
attempt to find out if patients experienced more life events just prior to
the onset of the depressive episode, and if so, if certain types of life event
were implicated. They found that eight life events were significantly
more common in the depressed patients. These included an increase in
arguments with spouse, marital separation, a change in working conditions, serious illness of the patient or a family member, and a move of
residence. Some of the potentially stressful events, such as being discharged from employment or having a business failure, were so uncom-
monly encountered that it was not possible to draw conclusions about
whether or not they are capable of precipitating a depressive episode.

It should be borne in mind that these findings are open to misinterpretation; they are correlational, not causal. Confirmation of the causal
connection depends on independent verifications. Despite the
common-sense appeal of the claims about the relation between stressful

events and illness, such verification cannot be foregone. For example, it is likely that the independent emergence of depression may cause or contribute to the occurrence of adverse life events. The direction of influence has to be determined.

Most of the events described in this original study and its successors were in the range of everyday experiences rather than catastrophic. As Paykel points out, most people are able to deal with these events without developing depression. "Some other factors must contribute to the development of depression."[22] Even if we accept the part played by these life events in precipitating an episode of depression, we are left with a great deal to explain. The unexplained variance falls, according to Paykel, "under the general rubric of vulnerability or predisposition."[23] Even when the life-events table is refined and improved, as Paykel and his colleagues have successfully done, one has to resort to factors that reside within the person – be they historical, biological, or both.

The Yale group constructed a refined list of the most stressful life events. The event that was perceived as being most stressful was the death of a child, closely followed by a very high rating for the death of a spouse. The next five stress events, in order of magnitude, were a prison sentence, the death of a family member, infidelity on the part of a spouse, financial difficulties, business failure, a discharge, miscarriage, and divorce. (In an interesting application of this new scale, Paykel showed that the conventional distinction between endogenous and neurotic depression is not reflected in different responses to stressful events. The patients in both depressive groups, endogenous and neurotic, reported comparable exposures to potentially stressful events before the episode in question occurred.)

Despite the admitted weaknesses of this methodology (e.g., crude scales, variations in temporal connections, open to causal misinterpretation), progress has been made. It has been shown that although the majority of depressive episodes are preceded by an increase in stressful life events, this association falls far short of providing an adequate explanation of the occurrence of depression. To quote Paykel's conclusion: "The proportion of variance in causation which can be attributed to the life event is relatively small. The event falls on some kind of fertile soil, and a host of factors modify the reaction to it. While it is easy to specify these factors in broad terms, their detailed interactions with events have not been adequately studied" (p. 161).

Broadly similar results were reported by Brown,[24] who studied depressive episodes in a group of British patients. In the nine months preceding the occurrence of the depressive episode, 42 percent of the patients had at least one markedly severe event, whereas only 13 percent of the community control subjects reported such an event. Even more compelling was the finding that in the three weeks before the onset of the depressive episode, no less than 51 percent of the patients (compared with 17 percent of the controls) had at least one serious event. Brown interpreted his results to mean that it is only the severely threatening events that are "causally implicated" in the onset of depression. As in the research carried out at Yale, this clear evidence of a connection between a significant life event and the onset of depression nevertheless leaves a good deal of unexplained variance.

In an interesting comparison, Brown made similar observations on a group of schizophrenic patients. The life events experienced by fifty patients in the three three months before the onset of a psychotic episode were compared with those of a control group of nonpsychotic people. The results of this intensive study were summarized: "The entire difference (between the two groups) appeared to occur in the three-week period immediately before onset: The rate of events was three times greater in this time than in the general population sample, but outside of these three weeks the rate was much the same in the two groups. In the three-week period immediately before onset, the rates were 88 and 22 events per 100 persons for the patient and comparison group, respectively. Sixty percent of patients had at least one event in this period compared with 20 percent in the comparison group."[25] A variety of life events appeared to be capable of precipitating an acute schizophrenic attack, but in most of them the patient was the main focus of the event, for example, a family quarrel about, or provoked by, the patient. These results, and those described for depressive patients, should not be interpreted incorrectly to mean that these life events are essential causes; rather they indicate that significant life events are capable of precipitating episodes of psychiatric breakdown. In the case of schizophrenia, there is a close temporal connection between the occurrence of the event and the breakdown, but this is less evident in the cases of depressive episodes. It is important to bear in mind that in all these studies a significant minority of control subjects coped successfully with life events of comparable significance. In cardiovascular research work, considerable progress has been made in identifying personal vulnerabilities and resistances,[26] and before long advances will be made in applying these lessons to stress in general.

The excursion from the laboratory into the natural environment that is exemplified in the research on "recent life events" is a welcome transition in many ways, even though it is purchased at the price of a loss in precision. The work has inevitably dealt with large categories of life events in which the subtleties may be lost, and individual differences in reactivity are threatened with drowning. As we have just seen, a significant minority of people cope satisfactorily with apparently stressful events. Attempts to make the research sufficiently flexible to encompass individual differences, and in particular differences in how we perceive stressful events, are now under way, and there is every reason to expect them to be productive. For example, Garmezy's ongoing research into how some children survive and even flourish under the most appalling conditions should provide valuable enlightenment.

Control

A useful guide to this emerging trend can be found in work of Seligman,[11] mentioned earlier. We draw attention to the fact that adequate preparation for potentially stressful events can be beneficial, and also noted that increased predictability of such events is inherently helpful. Our remarks on the relationship between *predictability* and the reduction or prevention of adverse responses to stressors are relevant not only to methods of preparing people psychologically for stressful medical experiences (see Chapter 11), but also have wider applicability. In the context of reactions to stress, the related concept of *controllability* is even more pertinent.

In the original formulation of Seligman's theory of helplessness, controllability was the key concept – "a person or animal is helpless with respect to some outcome when the outcome occurs independently of all of his voluntary responses" – the outcome is uncontrollable. According to Seligman, the sense of uncontrollability gives rise to three types of disruption. "The motivation to respond is sapped, the ability to perceive success is undermined, and emotionality is heightened."[27] These three types of disturbance can be grouped under the headings of motivation, emotion, and cognition. The theory, preferably in its expanded and revised form,[28] provides a useful framework for investigating the effects of potentially stressful events, and also holds the promise of leading to improved methods for preventing adverse effects or coping with those consequences that cannot be avoided. Stated in simple terms, practice or action that increases the person's sense of controllability in a threatening situation will help to prevent or mitigate potential stress. Although some exceptions were found, a reanalysis of the information on the stresses endured during World War II confirmed the applicability of the concept of controllability.[14] Broadly speaking, those soldiers and airmen who expressed great confidence in their skills and weapons reported fewer and less disruptive fears. The most important exception to the controllability explanation comes not from a military sample, but from the civilian

population. Contrary to expectation, comparatively few civilians developed serious problems or fears as a result of being exposed to the
unpredictability and uncontrollability of repeated air raids.[14] With increasing exposure to raids, people habituated instead of becoming sen-
sitized. The power of the habituation process presumably suppressed the
adverse effects of uncontrollable stressors.

Can stressors cause death?

In developing his theory, Seligman went as far as to argue that the
psychological state of helplessness can be lethal. "When animals and
men learn that their actions are futile and that there is no hope, they
become more susceptible to death. Conversely, the belief in control over
the environment can prolong life. . . the psychological state of helplessness increases risk of death."[29] After briefly reviewing some evidence on
sudden deaths observed in laboratory animals exposed to stress, Seligman
gathered from diverse sources anecdotal evidence suggesting that humans may be vulnerable to psychogenic death. The clinical anecdotes
are not always persuasive, but some of the anthropological evidence is
remarkable. Many trained and untrained anthropologists have described
the sudden and mysterious death of people accused and condemned by a
medicine man. It is agreed that these deaths by witchcraft, if that is what
they are, are bizarre and that they defy physiological explanation at
present. Seligman appears to be justified in insisting that these
phenomena should not be ignored, and his argument is strengthened by
some careful descriptions provided by Engel[30] and his colleagues at the
University of Rochester. In many of the 170 cases of sudden death
analyzed by this group, psychological factors appear to have played a
significant part. The loss of an important relative or friend by death, or
for other reasons, featured prominently in many cases. Other evidence[31]
strongly implicates the loss of close relatives in a variety of disorders
(e.g., strokes, hypertension), and these findings are of course consistent
with the drift of the argument. So too are the indications that psychological stresses can "increase the mortality of animals exposed to standardized doses of specific viruses or transplants of malignant tumors."[31]

The evidence collected so far is extremely interesting, but it is premature to conclude that psychological stress can cause deaths in human
beings. Nevertheless, it is worth bearing in mind that stressors can be an
indirect cause of death. A person who has a major dysfunction, such as a
cardiac disorder, is under greater risk when subjected to various forms of
stress than at other times. A direct connection is evident in cases of
self-inflicted death provoked or precipitated by a psychological event.

Suicide is almost always in some sense a stress-induced death, but it is not what psychologists usually have in mind when they ponder whether stress can cause death.

A better grasp of the events and circumstances that produce stressful effects is necessary in order to provide a firmer foundation on which to build a system of preventive behavioral medicine. But some useful progress has been made. There is little doubt about the stressful potential of unpredictable and uncontrollable aversive events. Preparation and rehearsal serve to reduce unpredictability and uncontrollability, and their value has been demonstrated in the research on preparing people for painful or unpleasant procedures. In chronic disorders, methods for helping patients to achieve greater control over, and competence in dealing with, their ailments and handicaps are bound to be valuable.

13 Projects and prospects

Plans for expanding the contributions made by psychologists to the theory and practice of medicine are less likely to meet frank opposition than concealed scepticism. Coming from a well-established profession with its victories on display, an open-minded scepticism toward the ambitions of the newer science of psychology should be accepted and even welcomed. It is largely up to psychologists to propose the plans and projects, to suggest ways in which their skills might be helpful.

Before discussing some of the practical obstacles to the infusion of psychology into medicine, we shall describe a selection of worthwhile projects that could be undertaken without delay (indeed, most of the topics have already been studied, to some extent). This "shopping list" is, of course, indicative, not comprehensive. Most of the ideas have been referred to earlier in this book and are presented as both reminder and prompt.

Psychologists could carry out surveys of existing infant and child welfare clinics and other services, in the hope of identifying the most serious and common psychological and behavior problems encountered by parents. In the light of this information, they could apply their extensive knowledge of child psychology and of behavior modification to dealing with these problems. Having established and evaluated the necessary methodology, they could work with the nursing, pediatric, and other personnel involved and greatly improve services. We are not referring here to psychiatric illnesses of childhood or even to what are regarded today as being psychiatric problems, but to the day to day, month to month problems of child development – social, intellectual, psychomotor, self-care, continence training, and the rest. Successful approaches to these problems would quickly grow into genuinely preventive forms of health care.

Pre-natal clinics are among the most common of the preventive medical services; they certainly provide the most intensive *preparation* for a medical experience. It is regrettable that this keen sense of the value of preparation has not been extended to other aspects of medical practice – perhaps repeated and convincing evaluations of pre-natal preparations may help to establish the *general* point in addition to the particular uses of pre-natal care. This assumes, of course, that the preparation is of value and, although indications are favorable, we need confirmation. In our view, any evaluation that neglects the significant psychological processes involved in the various stages of childbirth – from early pregnancy to at least three months after the birth – will be of limited value and potentially misleading. Given the requisite cooperation from the pregnant woman, pediatricians, and nurses, psychologists could make a helpful contribution here.

Admission to a hospital is a distressing experience for many people and especially the young. As long as we retain the view that emotional reactions in the hospital are a first-class annoyance, potentially or actually obstructing the investigatory or surgical procedures, they will continue to be just that – an obstructive nuisance. If, however, we remind ourselves that *medical care is not simply the search for cures, but fundamentally the alleviation of distress and pain – neither of which are solely "physical" phenomena – then emotional reactions to hospitals and illnesses are very much the business of medical practice.* As we have argued, there is good reason to believe (and even some slight evidence of a direct nature) that adequate preparation for hospitalization, and indeed for any painful or unusual investigations and procedures, is capable of reducing distress and aiding recovery. We have also argued that this preparation is primarily a psychological matter. Specific proposals for improving preparations for hospital admissions and operations are given in Chapter 11.

The relationship between a patient and his or her doctor, so much emphasized in the medical literature and teaching texts, apparently exerts a major influence on the outcome of consultations and any ensuing treatment. There can be no debate about the fact that the nature of this relationship is essentially a psychological subject (unfortunately neglected outside psychiatry). This fascinating phenomenon is extremely complex and has proved to be difficult to analyze in a scientific manner, but it can and should be studied – particularly, we feel, in the context of general practice. In the same province, the actual consultation session is in need of detailed examination. The value of these sessions is undoubtedly open to improvement. For example, we have referred to ways of improving doctors' communications with their patients. The powerful influence of well-delivered and timely advice from a doctor makes study of the consultation process as worthwhile as it is interesting.

In Chapter 7 we discussed the factors that contribute to the uncanny power of placebos; the patient's attitude to his or her doctor is a central factor, and psychologists could carry out a useful service by extending their study of placebo power from psychiatry into the whole range of medical practices. In view of the overwhelming use of pills and tablets in current practice, the great majority of consultations ending with the prescription of drugs, the importance of an increased understanding of the psychology of pill taking is self-evident.

The value of a satisfactory relationship between doctor and patient is suggested indirectly by the evidence on ways and means of giving up smoking, and presumably the relationship exerts a similar influence in related matters, such as avoiding certain foods, holding to diets, and so on. Psychological research into smoking behavior is well under way, but little attention has been given to ways of achieving the necessary restraints on unhealthy eating patterns, dieting, and the taking or avoiding of exercise (for example, in cases of cardiac disorder), and the many other behavioral prescriptions delivered by doctors. At first sight, none of them seems to pose any intellectual problems, and improved methods of self-control can be expected before long.

Matching compassion with energy, psychologists might in future try to redirect more care and attention toward the chronically ill and disabled, particularly to older people. Some work, but still far too little, has been carried out in caring for the aged ill, and in rehabilitation of blind or deaf people, among others. For psychologists, however, rehabilitation need not be confined to the tradition of occupational rehabilitation. Psychological rehabilitation should aim wider and include mobility and social and sexual adjustment, as well as a return to work. In many cases of handicap, chronic or sudden, the affected person needs to learn new ways of behaving, feeling, and relating to people. Medical rehabilitation centers should have a psychological service – even if psychologists themselves have first to show these establishments that they would benefit from a full service.

We need sensitive studies of the approach of death, including the taboos and profound fears attached to the subject. As a first step, it would be extremely valuable to have clarification of the question of doctors informing patients when they have a fatal illness. At present there seems to be a gulf between doctors and their patients, the former aiming to protect through ignorance and the patients resenting the concealment. Psychologists could play a major part in clearing up some of these problems, by working toward the identification of when to tell, whom to tell, and how to tell. There are few more distressing problems in the field of medicine than these, and they unquestionably need sympathetic and tactful study.

Doctors are, of course, also faced with the need to inform people of other types of misfortune, such as the diagnosis of crippling, chronic, and incurable illnesses. Investigation of these topics will presumably reveal the same gap between the wishes of the majority to be told the full facts and their doctors' reluctance to do so. Psychologists have made a start in analyzing why this reluctance occurs, and its consequences. Common explanations offered by doctors are that the information would cause unnecessary distress, or be misunderstood, or be resented – or all three. No doubt any and all of these reactions do occur, but it does not follow that silence or concealment are the only courses open. Working in collaboration with psychologists, doctors could develop methods of conveying news of misfortunes in a way that minimizes misunderstandings and comforts the distressed. We all need to learn a great deal more about how to help people to accept misfortune and how to cope with it; perhaps the progress made in reducing anxiety and depression will provide a helpful starting point. The beliefs that problems of death and misfortune cannot be studied in a detached manner and, further, that each doctor intuitively acts in the best way open to him or her, are not satisfactory. In dealing with these problems, doctors sometimes belittle themselves, not least by their inclination to deny that a significant reason for their reluctance to give painful news is that it is often a distressing and distasteful experience for them. Medical students and doctors could benefit from systematic preparation and counseling for this difficult part of their duties.

Professional cooperation: In a desire to contribute their knowledge and skills to medicine, psychologists may be inclined to exaggerate both – while losing sight of their ignorance of medical subjects. Somehow they need to achieve a balance between enthusiasm and humility. Whereas some doctors welcome cooperation from psychologists, others regard the notion with suspicion; the majority are likely to await events with one or other variety of scepticism. Some doctors fear that psychologists will intrude into the special relationship they have with their patients. Others are worried that, when psychologists work directly with patients, their own clinical responsibility may be eroded. These complex questions cannot be explored at length here, and although reassurance on the first fear is easily given, the fact is that psychologists and other health workers have already accepted a measure of clinical responsibility. Any person who gives a professional service to a patient assumes at least some clinical responsibility for his or her actions. Clinical responsibility is not a unitary concept, not a single indivisible lump. Each member of a medical team is responsible for his or her professional actions, and it is hard to see how it could be otherwise. It does not follow that doctors are losing in this process or that the interests of their patients are jeopardized. As the primary agents in the medical team, doctors usually have the main responsibility, and in any event, they need to ensure that their patients are assisted by suitably qualified and registered professionals.

We have devoted most of this chapter to proposals for psychological research, but the need for interprofessional cooperation is even greater in the service work provided in hospitals, clinics, and offices. Despite some persisting difficulties, psychologists and psychiatrists have established a useful clinical partnership, and one can easily foresee how mutually valuable working relationships could also grow between pediatricians and psychologists, neurologists and psychologists, and so on. Specialized clinics are among the most likely places for the growth of these contributory partnerships, and we can use pain clinics as an illustration. The neurologist and physician between them would arrive at a diagnosis and prescribe the necessary pills and/or surgery or whatever else is felt to be required. The persistence of the patient's pain in the face of these measures might signal the need for a more individual approach, taking into account his or her personality and present circumstances, understanding of the illness and the accompanying emotion, and so on. These are psychological matters, and their proper analysis might afford the patient some reassurance and comfort; in some cases, specific psychological methods might help to reduce the intensity and/or frequency of the pain, or modify the pain behavior, or increase or decrease pain complaints as necessary. Bearing in mind the more comprehensive theory of pain discussed in Chapter 4, there is good reason to hope that treatment directed at the upper, cognitive centers of the nervous system can benefit patients. Even in advance of a systematic attack on the problem, psychologists can offer several practical ideas for pain control. Anxiety-reduction methods will probably help some patients, especially those with neurotic and extraverted tendencies (who are known to complain more about their pains). The biofeedback method described in Chapter 8 is being turned toward the treatment of headaches and muscular pains, powerful suggestions (especially from a highly regarded doctor) can reduce pain; increased understanding and predictability of pain events can reduce subjective pain. There will be no shortages of ideas.

It would be a disservice to pretend that conflicts do not and will not occur, especially during the period of transition. The process of absorbing a new and vigorous science into the health service will be uncomfortable, even while it helps to improve patient care and invigorate the theory of medicine. As members of the more powerful and better established of the two disciplines, medical personnel can afford to be more accommodating and flexible – not an easy task for people educated in a firmly hierarchical profession. For their part, psychologists might avoid the pattern of grumbling grievances that surfaced from time to time in their psychiatric period. At the administrative planning level, the infusion of psychology into medicine will probably be achieved sooner and with fewer collisions if the provision of psychological services is organized and ordered at a very high level rather than within a single hospital or within small medical units. This is particularly desirable during the expected period of rapid change. Strategic planning can be carried out only at an executive level. The transfer of psychologists among projects, services, and specialities will require executive action, rather than a barter system within local hospitals.

Finally, it is well to remember that despite the conservative structure of their profession, doctors have shown themselves to be particularly responsive to useful clinical innovations.

Summing up: the potential benefits

Having urged a fundamental change in the scope of medical psychology, we must outline the benefits that might follow if our proposals were to be implemented.

Doctors can expect to benefit in three respects. The infusion of psychological influences into medical practice would certainly restore part of the human interest that has been drained away by the advances of technological medicine. These advances, combined with growing demands for medical help, reduce the time available for individual patients and also serve to limit each doctor's range of therapeutic service skills. Recognition of the important role of psychological factors in doctor-patient relationships, and their inevitable practical consequences, would help to restore the waning personal contacts of practicing doctors. It will, of course, entail spending more time with each patient as a prerequisite for relating to him or her as a person – bearing in mind that the patient, not the doctor, has the greatest responsibility for his or her own health. It will be objected, of course, that it is the doctor's *time* that is in shortest supply at present, and that to ask for more of it is absurdly unrealistic. So it is; if the prevailing forms of practice continue unaltered, there is little hope of nurturing the desired psychological relations between patient and doctor. In our view, medical practice *can* change in the desired direction, and time can be found for more personal consultations and exchanges. Our two suggestions are neither novel nor exclusive and, worse luck, they cannot be introduced quickly.

In the first place, a concerted program of health education should be undertaken in order to train all of us to accept greater responsibility for our own bodies; doctors need be consulted only when signs of serious difficulty appear. We know that the majority of visits made to family doctors are for minor pains, coughs, colds, and the like. These visits can be greatly reduced by education, given intensively at school and through the media, which would explain basic human physiology and the signs and symptoms of the statistically most common complaints. People could be told, clearly and often, when to seek professional help and what to do before it arrives or instead of it. In addition to public education, doctors need to do even more to educate their own patients and return some responsibility to them. Both private and public education would inevitably help to diminish those persisting aspects of medical paternalism, while helping to reverse the steadily increasing demands for medical help.

Second, the trends toward developing more and better ancillary workers can be accelerated. They can relieve doctors of part of their extensive clinical commitments in order to restore more *intensive* and prolonged therapeutic relationships. This book has indicated numerous ways, direct and indirect, in which psychologists can help doctors to cope with clinical demands. The most obvious and easily implemented of the direct psychological services include those pertaining to developmental and behavioral problems of childhood, sexual problems, sleep disorders and mild anxiety. Indirect help can be given by improving the treatment and control of pain (including headaches), adherence to medical advice, drug prescribing and imbibing on a more rational basis, and so on.

Psychology can also benefit medicine as a whole. Psychologists bring new conceptual tools to the task of developing adequate theories of illness and pain and their alleviation; they can add a great deal to our idea of the sick role, and to ideas about the nature of insanity and how it differs from behavior disorders. Their special skills can be applied to the analysis of doctors' feelings and behavior, patients' expectations, satisfactions, and dissatisfactions, and their relations. Psychologists, by view of the emphasis placed on research in the psychology syllabus, have a particularly helpful contribution to make to the solution of some critical problems in medicine; they need merely to receive an invitation.

Patients could profit from the greater use of psychology and psychologists in a general way – through the elevation of standards of care – and in a special way, from a widening of our conception of what patients should receive from their doctors. In addition to skilled technical aid, patients need comfort and sympathy, preferably of a nonpaternalistic brand. People want more information about their ailments, the tests they undergo, the drugs they take, their prognosis. All of these needs and wants are far more likely to be met by doctors who are trained to recognize their patients' psychological requirements as well as their bodily dysfunctions. Patients would experience less pain and less distress if they were given adequate preparation for operations, investigations, and hospital admissions – and "adequate preparation" is primarily a psychological matter.

Acceptance of our broader view of the role of psychologists in medicine would benefit them immeasurably. Indeed, it is our opinion that unless psychologists take up these new challenges, their profession is unlikely to attain maturity. There is little to be said, either professionally or intellectually, for a highly trained group of people choosing to remain in the shadow of a single specialized branch of medicine. If they aspire to be junior psychiatrists, or junior doctors of any sort, psychologists are bound to be worn by perpetual frustration, while at the same time arousing the worst suspicions in their medical colleagues. Psychologists are sometimes accused of wishing to act like doctors, and worse, of wanting to further this ambition deviously. It can be admitted that some (many?) clinical psychologists are frustrated doctors, but within the new framework for psychology and medicine proposed here they could more than satisfy their not ignoble ambitions. Insofar as they share with members of the medical profession a desire to relieve distress and provide comfort for people in difficulty, there will be ample opportunity for them to work toward their aims. What distinguishes their speciality is the central importance of psychological factors. If psychologists with medical interests insist on working their own ground – the subjective, behavioral and psychophysiological aspects of health and sickness – the next decade could be by far the most rewarding and exciting in the history of their emerging profession.

Notes

Foreword

1. Neal Miller, Behavioral Medicine: New Opportunities but Serious Dangers, *Behavioral Medicine Update*, 1, 5 (1979).

1 *Introduction*

1. W. Glazier, The Task of Medicine, *Scientific American*, **228**, 13–17 (1973).
2. V. Fuchs, *Who Shall Live?*, Basic Books, New York, 1974.
3. R. Melzack, *The Puzzle of Pain*, Penguin Books, Harmondsworth, England, 1973.
4. A. Cochrane, *Effectiveness and Efficiency*, Nuffield Provincial Hospitals Trust, London, 1972.
5. M. Stacey, R. Dearden, R. Pill, and D. Robinson, *Hospitals, Children and Their Families*, Routledge & Kegan Paul, London, 1970.
6. W. Liston and A. Campbell, *British Medical Journal*, **iii**, 606 (1974).
7. *Lancet*, editorial, November 16, 1974.
8. *The (London) Times*, June 30, 1976, p. 4.
9. Donald Gould, *New Scientist*, June 10, 1976, pp. 598–9.

2 *Psychology and behavioral medicine*

1. Office of Health Economics, *Medicine and Society*, no. 43 (1972).
2. M. Shepherd, S. Mitchell, and B. Oppenheim, *Childhood Behaviour and Mental Health*, London University Press, London, 1971.
3. H. J. Eysenck and S. Rachman, *Bulletin of the British Psychological Society*, **26**, 1130 (1973).
4. R. Hetherington, *Bulletin of the British Psychological Society*, **20**, 1 (1967).
5. P. Ley, *Bulletin of the British Psychological Society*, **25**, 115 (1972).
6. P. Ley, *Proceedings of the British Association for the Advancement of Science*, September 1971.
7. G. Patterson and M. Gullion, *Living with Children*, Research Press, Champaign, Ill. 1972.
8. G. Patterson, *Families*, Research Press, Champaign, Ill., 1971.
9. L. Hoffman and M. Hoffman, *Review of Child Development Research*, 1 and 2, Russell Sage Fund, New York, 1964 and 1966.

3 Doctor's orders

1. B. Korsch and V. Negrete, Scientific American, **227,** 66 (1972).
2. P. Ley, Bulletin of British Psychological Society, **25** 115, (1972).
3. P. Ley, Psychological Studies of Doctor-Patient Communication, in S. Rachman (ed.), Contributions to Medical Psychology, Vol. I, Pergamon Press, Oxford, 1977.
4. C. Fletcher, Communication in Medicine, Nuffield Hospital Trust, London, 1973.
5. J. Aitken-Swan and E. Easson, British Medical Journal, **1,** 779 (1959).
6. P. Ley and S. Spelman, Communicating with the Patient, Staples Press, 1967.
7. R. K. Turner, G. Young, and S. Rachman, Behaviour Research and Therapy, **8,** 367 (1970).
8. D. Sackett, R. Haynes, E. Gibson, B. Hackett, D. Taylor, R. Roberts, and A. Johnson, Lancet, **i,** 1205 (1976).
9. R. B. Haynes, D. Sackett, E. Gibson, D. Taylor, B. Hackett, R. Roberts, and A. Johnson, Lancet, **i,** 1265 (1976).
10. P. Ley, Psychological Medicine, **3,** 217 (1973).
11. H. Williams, The Practitioner, 202 (1969).
12. H. Leventhal, L. Berkowitz (ed.), Advances in Experimental Social Psychology, Academic Press, New York, 1970.
13. I. Janis and S. Feshbach, Journal of Abnormal and Social Psychology, **48,** 78 (1953).
14. H. Leventhal, J. Watts, and F. Pagano, Journal of Personality and Social Psychology, **6,** 313 (1967).
15. S. Rachman, Bibliotheca Nutritio, et Dieta, No. 14, Malnutrition Is a Problem of Ecology, G. György (ed.), 1970.
16. A. Tesser and S. Rosen, in L. Berkowitz (ed.), Advances in Experimental Social Psychology, Academic Press, New York, 1975.
17. E. Saul and J. Kass, Journal of Medical Education, **44,** 526 (1969).

4 Pain

1. R. Melzack, The Puzzle of Pain, Penguin Books, Harmondsworth, England, 1973.
2. H. K. Beecher, Measurement of Subjective Responses, Oxford University Press, London, 1959.
3. W. K. Livingstone, Pain Mechanisms, Macmillan, New York, 1943.
4. M. Weisenberg, Psychological Bulletin, **84**(5), 1008–44 (1977).
5. P. Wall, Brain, **101,** 1 (1978).
6. R. Melzack, A. Z. Wetsz, and L. T. Sprague, Experimental Neurology, **8,** 239 (1963).
7. S. B. Cheng and L. K. Ding, Nature, April 27, 1973, p. 242.
8. R. Melzack, Pain, **3,** 3–23 (1977).

9. H. Merskey, unpublished thesis, Oxford University, 1964.
10. M. Hunter, C. Philips, and S. Rachman, *Pain*, **6**, 35 (1979).
11. M. R. Bond and I. Pilowsky, *Journal of Psychosomatic Research*, **10**, 203 (1966).
12. J. D. Hardy, H. G. Wolff, and H. Goodell, *Pain Sensations and Reactions*, Williams & Wilkins, New York, 1952.
13. K. Woodrow, G. Friedman, A. Siegelaub, and M. Collen, *Psychosomatic Medicine*, **34**, 548 (1972).
14. I. Janis, *Stress and Frustration*, Harcourt Brace, New York, 1971, chap. 9.
15. M. R. Bond, *British Journal of Psychiatry*, **199**, 553 (1971).
16. R. Lynn and H. J. Eysenck, *Perceptual and Motor Skills*, **12**, 161–2 (1961).
17. S. B. G. Eysenck, *Journal of Mental Science*, **107**, 417–30 (1961).
18. A. Petrie, *Individuality in Pain and Suffering*, University of Chicago Press, Chicago, 1967.
19. H. J. Eysenck, *The Biological Basis of Personality*, Charles C. Thomas, Springfield, Ill., 1971.
20. W. E. Fordyce, R. S. Fowler, and B. Delateur, *Behaviour Research and Therapy*, **6**, 105–7 (1968).

5 A psychological approach to headaches

1. W. E. Waters, *Headache*, **4**, 178–86 (1970).
2. A. M. Ostfeld, *The Common Headache Syndromes: Biochemistry, Pathophysiology, Therapy*, Charles C Thomas, Springfield, Ill., 1962.
3. B. Chew, *British Office of Health Economics*, personal communication, 1979.
4. R. Kohn and K. White (eds.), *Health Care: An International Study*, Oxford University Press, London, 1976.
5. H. G. Wolff, *Headache and Other Head Pain*, Oxford University Press, London, 1963.
6. A. P. Friedman, *Journal of the American Medical Association*, **179**, 717–18 (1962).
7. A. P. Friedman, *Neurology*, **4**, 773–88 (1964).
8. A. P. Friedman, *Journal of the American Medical Association*, **190**, 445–7 (1964).
9. W. E. Waters, *British Medical Journal*, **2**, 77–81 (1971).
10. P. Sainsbury and J. G. Gibson, *Journal of Neurology, Neurosurgery and Psychiatry*, **17**, 216 (1954).
11. H. C. Philips, A Psychological Analysis of Tension Headaches, in S. Rachman (ed.), *Contributions to Medical Psychology, Vol. I*, Pergamon Press, Oxford, 1977.
12. H. C. Philips, *Behaviour Research and Therapy*, **16**, 249–61 (1978).
13. L. M. Epstein, G. Abel, F. Collins, L. Parker, and P. Cinciripini, *Behaviour Research and Therapy*, **16**, 153–60 (1978).

14. H. Selensky, *Bulletin of the New York Academy of Medicine*, **15**, 757 (1939).
15. M. J. Martin and P. Rome, in A. P. Friedman (ed.), *Studies in Headache—Research and Clinical*, Vol. 1, Karger, Basle, 1967.
16. A. P. Friedman, *Headaches*, in Comprehensive Textbook of Psychiatry, Vol. 2., edited by A. M. Freedman et al., Williams & Wilkins, Baltimore, 1974.
17. H. C. Philips, *J. Psychosomatic Research*, **20**, 535 (1976).
18. H. J. Eysenck and S. B. G. Eysenck, *Manual of Eysenck Personality Questionnaire*, Hodder and Stoughton, London, 1976.
19. H. Merskey and D. Boyd, *Pain*, **4**, 174–9 (1978).
20. S. Rodbard, Pain in Contracting Muscle, in J. Crue (ed.), *Pain-Research and Treatment*, Academic Press, New York, 1975.
21. A. M. Ostfeld, *American Journal of Medical Sciences*, **241**, 192 (1961)
22. A. P. Friedman and H. Merritt, *Journal of the American Medical Association*, **163**, 1111 (1957).
23. A. P. Friedman, *Neurology*, **13**, 27–33 (1963).
24. S. Diamond, in D. Appenzeller (ed.), *Psychogenic Headache, Pathogenesis and Treatment of Headache*, Spectrum Publications, New York, 1976.
25. R. Delaplaine, O. Ifabumuyi, H. Mersky, and J. Zarfas, *Pain*, **4**, 361–6 (1978).
26. O. Appenzeller, K. Davidson, and J. Marshall, *Journal of Neurology, Neurosurgery and Psychiatry*, **26**, 447 (1962).
27. I. D. Balshan, *Archives of General Psychiatry*, **7**, 436–48 (1962).
28. R. Melzack and W. S. Torgenson, *Anaesthesiology*, **34**, 50 (1971).
29. H. C. Philips, *Headache*, **16**, 322, 1977.
30. S. Rachman, *The Meanings of Fear*, Penguin Books, Harmondsworth, England, 1974; and *Fear and Courage*, Freemans, San Francisco, 1978.
31. H. C. Philips, *Behaviour Research and Therapy*, **15**, 119 (1977).
32. W. E. Fordyce, R. S. Fowler, and B. Delateur, *Behaviour Research and Therapy*, **6**, 105–7 (1968).
33. D. Bakal, *Psychological Bulletin*, **82**, 367–83 (1975).

6 Sleep disorders

1. K. Dunnell and A. Cartwright, *Medicine Takers, Prescribers and Hoarders*, Routledge & Kegan Paul, London, 1972.
2. M. Shepherd, B. Cooper, A. Brown, and G. Kelkon, *Psychiatric Illness in General Practice*, Oxford University Press, 1966.
3. T. D. Borkovec, Pseudo (Experiential) Insomnia and Idiopathic (Objective) Insomnia: Theoretical and Therapeutic Issues, *Advances in Behavior Research*, **2**, 27, (1979).
4. (British) *Office of Health Economics*, personal communication, 1979.
5. (British) *Office of Health Economics, Compendium of Health Statistics*, 2nd ed., 1977.
6. D. Dunlop, *British Medical Bulletin*, **26**, 236 (1970).

7. H. G. Jones, and I. Oswald, *Electroencephalography and Clinical Neurophysiology*, **24**, 378 (1968).

8. I. Oswald, *Sleep*, Penguin Books, Harmondsworth, England, 1966.

9. N. Kleitman, *Sleep and Wakefulness*, University of Chicago Press, Chicago, 1963.

10. H. L. Williams and C. Williams, *Psychophysiology*, **3**, 164–75 (1966).

11. R. T. Wilkinson, in L. A. Abt and B. F. Reiss (eds.), *Progress in Clinical Psychology*, Grune & Stratton, New York, 1969.

12. A. Kales, *Sleep: Physiology and Pathology*, J. B. Lippincott, New York, 1969.

13. A. Kales and J. Kales, in G. Madin (ed.), *Recent Advances in Diagnosis and Treatment of Sleep Disorders, Sleep Research and Clinical Practice*, Brunner/Mazel, New York, 1973.

14. D. R. Hawkins, in E. Hartmann (ed.), *Sleep and Dreaming*, Little, Brown, Boston, 1970.

15. P. Hauri, in E. Hartmann (ed.), *Sleep and Dreaming*, Little, Brown, Boston, 1970.

16. B. A. Schwartz, G. Guilband, and H. Fischgeld, *Presse Medicine*, **71,** 1474 (1963).

17. L. J. Monroe, *Journal of Abnormal Psychology*, **74,** 255 (1967).

18. T. D. Borkovec and D. C. Fowles, *Journal of Abnormal Psychology*, **1,** 153–8 (1973).

19. S. W. Steinmark and T. D. Borkovec, in T. D. Borkovec and D. A. Bernstein (eds.), *Progressive Relaxation Training*, Research Press, Ill., 1973.

20. R. Turner, G. Young, and S. Rachman, *Behaviour Research and Therapy*, **8,** 376 (1970).

21. B. Hallgren, *Acta Psychiatrica et Neurologica (Scandinavia)*, **31,** 379 (1956).

22. R. Lapouse and M. Monk, *American Journal of Orthopsychiatry*, **29,** 803 (1959).

23. A. MacFarlane, L. Allen, and M. Honzik, *A Developmental Study of Behavior Problems in Normal Children*, University of California Press, San Francisco, 1954.

24. S. Lovibond, *Conditioning and Enuresis*, Pergamon Press, Oxford, 1964.

25. G. Young and R. K. Turner, *Health and Social Service Journal*, April 1973, p. 793.

26. G. DeLeon and W. Mandell, *Journal of Clinical Psychology*, **22,** 326 (1966).

27. J. Werry and J. Cohrssen, *Journal of Pediatrics*, **67,** 423 (1965).

28. H. G. Jones, in H. J. Eysenck (ed.), *Behaviour Therapy and the Neuroses*, Pergamon Press, Oxford, 1960.

29. H. J. Eysenck and S. Rachman, *Causes and Cures of Neurosis*, Routledge & Kegan Paul, London, 1965.

30. R. K. Turner, G. Young, and S. Rachman, *Behavior Research and Therapy*, **8,** 376 (1970).

31. W. Finley, R. Besserman, L. Bennett, R. Clapp, and P. Finley, *Behaviour Research and Therapy*, **11,** 289 (1973).

32. C. Fisher, J. Byrne, A. Edwards, and E. Kahn, *Journal of American Psychoanalytic Association*, **18**, 4 (1970).

7 *Placebo power*

1. K. Dunnell and A. Cartwright, *Medicine Takers, Prescribers and Hoarders*, Routledge & Kegan Paul, London 1972.
2. D. Dunlop, *British Medical Bulletin*, **26**, 236–9 (1970).
3. O. Wade, *British Medical Bulletin*, **26**, 240 (1970).
4. D. Rosenhan, *Science*, **179**, 250 (1973).
5. R. Bell, *Woman in Health and Sickness*, 5th ed., Newnes, London, 1923.
6. A. Miller, M. Phil. dissertation, University of London, 1973.
7. N. Brill, *Archives of General Psychiatry*, **10**, 581 (1964).
8. L. Park and L. Covi, *Archives of General Psychiatry*, **12**, 336 (1965).
9. A. Shapiro, in A. Bergin and S. Garfield (eds.), *Handbook of Psychotherapy and Behavior Change*, John Wiley, New York, 1971, chap. 12. See also the second edition (1978).
10. J. Frank, *Persuasion and Healing*, rev. ed., Johns Hopkins University Press, Baltimore, 1973.
11. G. Paul, *Insight Versus Desensitization*, Stanford University Press, Stanford, Calif., 1966.
12. G. Young and R. Turner, *Behaviour Research and Therapy*, **3**, 93 (1965).
13. C. Joyce, *Proceedings of the Royal Society of Medicine*, **55**, 776 (1962).
14. G. Foulds, *Journal of Mental Science*, **104**, 259 (1958).
15. G. Uhlenhuth et al., *American Journal of Psychiatry*, **115**, 905 (1959).

8 *Self-control of bodily functions*

1. N. E. Miller, *Science*, **163**, 434–45 (1969).
2. N. E. Miller, *Annual Review of Psychology*, **29**, 373–404 (1978).
3. M. Wenger and B. Bajchi, *Behavioral Science*, **6**, 312–23 (1961).
4. A. Koestler, *The Lotus and the Robot*, Hutchinson, London 1960.
5. N. E. Miller, in T. X. Barber, L. V. DiCara, J. Kamiya, N. Miller, D. Shapiro, and J. Stoyva (eds.), *Biofeedback and Self-Control*, Aldine, Chicago 1970.
6. P. Lang, in P. Obrist, P. Black, J. Brewer, and L. V. DiCara (eds.), *Cardiovascular Psychophysiology*, Aldine, Chicago, 1974.
7. P. Lang and C. Twentyman, *Psychophysiology*, **11**, 616–29 (1974).
8. P. Lang, personal communication, 1976.
9. J. Brener, Sensory and Perceptual Determinants of Voluntary Visceral Control, in G. E. Schwartz and J. Beatty (eds.), *Biofeedback: Theory and Research*, Academic Press, New York, 1977.
10. J. Brener, in J. DiCara (ed.), *Limbic and Autonomic Nervous System Research*, Plenum Publishing Co., New York, 1974.

11. N. Miller and B. Dworkin, in P. Obrist, P. Black, J. Brewer, and L. V. DiCara (eds.), *Cardiovascular Psychophysiology*, Chicago, 1974.
12. A. H. Harris and J. V. Brady, *Annual Review of Psychology*, **25**, 107–33 (1974).
13. P. Lang, *Psychosomatic Medicine*, **37**, 429–46 (1975).
14. M. W. Headrick, B. W. Feather, and D. T. Wells, *Psychophysiology*, **8**, 132–42 (1971).
15. D. Shapiro and G. Schwartz, *Psychophysiology*, **9**, 296–304 (1972).
16. D. Shapiro, B. Tursky, and G. E. Schwartz, *Psychosomatic Medicine*, **32**, 417–23 (1970).
17. H. D. Kimmel, *Psychological Bulletin*, **67**, 337–45 (1967).
18. J. V. Basmajian, *Science*, **141**, 440–1 (1963).
19. P. B. Fenwick, *Electroencephalography and Clinical Neurophysiology*, **21**, 618 (1966).
20. A. Maslow, *American Psychologist*, **24**, 724–35 (1969).
21. E. Blanchard and L. Young, *Archives of General Psychiatry*, **30**, 573–589 (1974).
22. T. Weiss and B. T. Engel, *Psychosomatic Medicine*, **33**(4), 301–23 (1971).
23. B. T. Engel, Operant Conditioning of Cardiovascular Function, in S. Rachman (ed.), *Contributions to Medical Psychology*, Vol. I, Pergamon Press, Oxford, 1977.
24. B. Shapiro, H. Benson, B. Tursky, and G. E. Schwartz, *Science*, **173**, 740–2 (1971).
25. S. Elder and Z. Rviz, *Journal Applied Behavioral Analysis*, **6**, 377–82 (1973).
26. T. H. Budzynski, *Journal of Behavior Therapy and Experimental Psychiatry*, **1**, 202–11 (1970).
27. T. H. Budzynski, J. M. Stoyva, and C. Adler, *Psychosomatic Medicine*, **35**, 484–96 (1975).
28. D. F. Hutchings and R. Reinking, *Biofeedback and Self Regulation*, **1**, 183 (1976).
29. E. B. Blanchard, Biofeedback and Modification of Cardiovascular Dysfunctions, in J. Gatchel and K. P. Price (eds.), *Clinical Applications of Biofeedback: Appraisal and Status*, Pergamon Press, Elmsford, New York, 1979.
30. A. Jacob and R. Felton, *Archives of Physical Medicine*, **50**, 34–9 (1969).

9 Reducing health risks by self-control

1. M. Russell, *Nursing Times*, May 1972, p. 95.
2. E. Abramson, *Behaviour Research and Therapy*, **12**, 1974.
3. A. McKennell and R. Thomas, *Adults and Adolescents' Smoking Habits and Attitudes*, Her Majesty's Stationery Office, London, 1967.
4. J. Bynner, *The Young Smoker*, Her Majesty's Stationery Office, London, 1969.
5. M. Russell, *British Medical Journal*, **2**, 330 (1971).

6. M. Russell, *British Journal of Medical Psychology*, **44**, 1–16 (1971).
7. W. Dunn, *Smoking Behavior*, Winston, Washington, D.C., 1973.
8. H. J. Eysenck, *Personality and the Maintenance of the Smoking Habit* in W. Dunn (ed.), *Smoking Behavior*, Winston, Washington, D.C., 1977.
9. D. Bernstein, *Psychological Bulletin*, **71**, 418 (1969).
10. S. Rachman, *Bibliotheca Nutritia et Dieta*, **14**, 132 (1970).
11. M. Russell, *British Medical Journal*, **1**, 82 (1970).
12. M. Russell, E. Armstrong, and U. Patel, *Behaviour Research and Therapy*, **14**, 103 (1976).
13. P. Boudewyns, in R. Williams and W. Gentry (eds.), *Behavioral Approaches to Medical Treatment*, Ballinger, Cambridge, 1977.
14. M. Raw, in S. Rachman (eds.), *Contributions to Medical psychology*, Vol. I, Pergamon Press, Oxford, 1977.
15. H. Williams, *The Practitioner*, **202**, 672 (1969).
16. A. Stunkard, New York Journal of Medicine, **58**, 147 (1958).
17. S. Schachter, *American Psychologist*, **26**, 129 (1971).
18. S. Schachter, *Emotion, Obesity and Crime*, Academic Press, New York, 1971.
19. C. Ferster, C. Nurnberger, and E. Levitt, *Journal of Mathetics*, **1**, 129 (1962).
20. R. Stuart, *Behaviour Research and Therapy*, **5**, 357 (1967).
21. R. Stuart, *Behaviour Research and Therapy*, **9**, 177 (1971).
22. J. Foreyt (ed.), *Behavioral Treatments for Obesity*, Pergamon Press, Oxford, 1976.
23. S. Penick et al., *Psychosomatic Medicine*, **33**, 49 (1971).

10 Psychiatric psychology

1. J. Zubin, L. Efron, and F. Schumer, *An Experimental Approach to Projective Tests*, John Wiley, New York, 1965.
2. H. J. Eysenck in G. Fleming (ed.), *Recent Advances in Psychiatry*, Churchill, London, 1958.
3. K. Little and E. Shneidman, *Psychological Monographs*, **73**, no. 476 (1959).
4. S. Rachman, *The Effects of Psychotherapy*, Pergamon Press, 1971. See also 2nd ed., by Rachman and Wilson, 1980.
5. C. Rogers, *Journal of Consulting Psychology*, **21**, 95 (1957).
6. S. Rachman, *Psychological Bulletin*, **67**, 93 (1967).
7. H. J. Eysenck (ed.), *Behaviour Therapy and the Neuroses*, Pergamon Press, Oxford, 1969; and H. J. Eysenck (ed.), *Case Studies in Behaviour Therapy*, Routledge & Kegan Paul, London, 1976.
8. A. Kazdin and G. T. Wilson, *Evaluation of Behavior Therapy*, Ballinger, Cambridge, 1978.
9. S. Rachman and J. Teasdale, *Aversion Therapy and Behaviour Disorders*, Routledge & Kegan Paul, London, 1969.

10. I. Marks, *Fears and Phobias,* Heinemann, London, 1969.
11. V. Meyer and E. Chesser, *Behaviour Therapy in Clinical Psychiatry,* Penguin Books, Harmondsworth, England, 1970.
12. M. P. Feldman and A. Broadhurst (eds.), *Theoretical and Experimental Bases of the Behaviour Therapies,* John Wiley, New York, 1976.
13. R. Kendell, *British Journal of Hospital Medicine,* **6,** 147 (1971).
14. S. Rachman, *New Society,* April 1973, p. 793.
15. M. P. Seligman, *Helplessness,* W. H. Freeman, San Francisco, 1975.
16. L. Abramson, M. Seligman, and J. Teasdale, *Journal of Abnormal Psychology,* **87,** 49 (1978).
17. A. Bergin, in A. Bergin and S. Garfield (eds.), *Handbook of Psychotherapy and Behavior Change,* John Wiley, New York, 1971.
18. J. Frank, in R. Porter (ed.), *The Role of Learning in Psychotherapy,* Churchill, London, 1968.
19. S. Rachman and R. Hodgson, *Obsessions and Compulsions,* Prentice-Hall, Englewood Cliffs, N.J. 1980.
20. A. Bandura, *The Principles of Behavior Modification,* Holt, Rinehart & Winston, New York, 1969.
21. Memorandum of a Working Party set up by the Royal College of Psychiatrists, *British Journal of Psychiatry,* **1,** 123 (1973).
22. D. Rosenhan, *Science,* **179,** 250 (1973).

11. *The psychological impact of hospitalization*

1. I. Janis, *Stress and Frustration,* Harcourt Brace, New York, 1971.
2. P. Ley, In S. Rachman (ed.), *Contributions to Medical Psychology,* Vol. I, Pergamon Press, Oxford, 1977.
3. B. Melamed, in S. Rachman (ed.), *Contributions to Medical Psychology,* Vol. I, I, Pergamon Press, Oxford, 1977.
4. R. Lazarus, *Psychological Stress and the Coping Process,* McGraw-Hill, New York, 1966.
5. S. Rachman, *Fear and Courage,* W. H. Freeman, San Francisco, 1978.
6. L. Egbert, G. Battit, C. Welch, and M. Bartlett, *New England Journal of Medicine,* **270,** 825 (1964).
7. T. Morris, S. Greer, and P. White, *Cancer,* **40,** 2381 (1977).
8. J. John, in A. Rogers (ed.), *Exploring Progress in Medical-Surgical Nursing,* American Nursing Association, New York, 1965.
9. F. Schmitt and P. Woolridge, *Nursing Research,* **22,** 108 (1973).
10. R. Davie, N. Butler, and H. Goldstein, *From Birth to Seven,* Longmans, London, 1972.
11. *Lancet,* editorial, **2,** 1292 (1967).
12. B. Wood, Y. Wong, and C. Theodoridis, *Lancet,* **2,** 645 (1972).
13. M. Rutter, *Maternal Deprivation Reassessed,* Penguin Books, Harmondsworth, England, 1972.

14. L. Yarrow, in L. and E. Hoffman (eds.), *Review of Child Development Research*, Russell Sage Foundation, New York, 1964.
15. M. Stacey, R. Dearden, R. Pill, and D. Robinson, *Hospitals, Children and their Families*, Routledge & Kegan Paul, London, 1970.
16. S. Rachman, in M. P. Feldman and A. Broadhurst (eds.), *Theoretical and Experimental Foundations of the Behaviour Therapies*, John Wiley, New York, 1976.
17. D. Prugh et al., *American Journal of Orthopsychiatry*, **23**, 70 (1953).
18. P. Moran, thesis, Yale University, 1963, quoted by Janis (see note 1).
19. B. G. Melamed, in S. Rachman (ed.), *Contributions to Medical Psychology*, Vol. I, Pergamon Press, Oxford, 1977.
20. B. Melamed and L. Seigel, *Journal of Consulting Clinical Psychology*, **43**, 511 (1975).
21. B. Melamed et al., *Journal of the American Dental Association*, **90**, 822 (1975).
22. M. Seligman, *Helplessness*, W. H. Freeman, San Francisco, 1975.
23. S. Mineka and J. Kihlström, *Journal of Abnormal Psychology*, **87**, 256 (1978).
24. D. Vernon et al., *The Psychological Responses of Children to Hospitalization and Illness*, Charles C Thomas, Springfield, Ill., 1965.

12 Health and stress

1. I. Janis, *Stress and Frustration*, Harcourt Brace, New York, 1971.
2. A. Lewis, *Lancet*, **2**, 175 (1942).
3. B. Houston, L. Bloom, T. Burish, and E. Cummings, *Journal of Personality*, **46**, 205 (1978).
4. D. Broadbent, *Decision and Stress*, Academic Press, New York, 1971.
5. W. H. Gantt, *Psychosomatic Medicine Monographs*, nos. 3 and 4 (1944).
6. P. Broadhurst, in H. J. Eysenck (ed.), *Handbook of Abnormal Psychology*, Pitmans, London, 1970.
7. H. Liddell, in J. McV. Hunt (ed.) *Personality and the Behavior Disorders*, Ronald Press, New York, 1944.
8. J. Wolpe, *Psychotherapy by Reciprocal Inhibition*, Stanford University Press, Stanford, Calif., 1958.
9. J. Weiss, in J. Maser and M. Seligman (eds.), *Psychopathology: Experimental Models*, W. H. Freeman, San Francisco, 1977.
10. S. Mineka and J. Kihlström, *Journal of Abnormal Psychology*, **87**, 256 (1978).
1. J. Weiss, *Psychosomatic Medicine*, **32**, 397 (1970).
12. M. Seligman, *Helplessness*, W. H. Freeman, San Francisco, 1975.
13. A. Bandura, *Psychological Review*, **84**, 191 (1977).
14. S. Rachman, *Fear and Courage*, W. H. Freeman, San Francisco, 1978.
15. S. Stouffer, A. Lumsdaine, M. Lumsdaine, R. Williams, M. Smith, I. Janis, S. Star, and L. Cottrell, *The American Soldier*, Princeton University Press, Princeton, N.J., 1948, p. 225.
16. T. Holmes and R. Rahe, *Journal of Psychosomatic Research*, **8**, 35 (1964).

17. R. Rahe, *Journal of Human Stress*, **4,** 3 (1978).
18. R. Rahe, in E. Gunderson and R. Rahe (eds.), *Life Stress and Illness*, Charles C Thomas, Springfield, Ill., 1974.
19. Rahe, ibid., p. 58.
20. Rahe, ibid., p. 70.
21. E. Paykel, in E. Gunderson and R. Rahe, *Life Stress and Illness*, Charles C Thomas, Springfield, Ill., 1974.
22. Paykel, ibid., p. 143.
23. Paykel, ibid., pp. 146, 147.
24. G. Brown, in E. Gunderson and R. Rahe,(eds.), in *Life Stress and Illness*, Charles C Thomas, Springfield, Ill., 1974.
25. Brown, ibid., p. 171.
26. R. Suinn, in R. Williams and W. Gentry (eds.), *Behavioral Approaches to Medical Treatment*, Ballinger, Cambridge, 1977.
27. M. Seligman, *Helplessness*, W. H. Freeman, San Francisco, 1975, p. 44.
28. L. Abramson, M. Seligman and J. Teasdale, *Journal of Abnormal Psychology*, vol. 87, 1978, 49.
29. M. Seligman, *Helplessness*, W. H. Freeman, San Francisco, 1975, p. 168.
30. G. Engel, *Annals of International Medicine*, **74,** 771 (1971).
31. N. Miller, in A. Freedman, H. Kaplan, and B. Sadock (eds.), *Comprehensive Textbook of Psychiatry*, 2nd ed., Williams & Wilkins, Baltimore, 1974.

Suggestions for further reading

1 Introduction

Journal of Behavioral Medicine, edited by W. D. Gentry, Plenum Press, New York, successive issues.

S. Rachman (ed.), *Contributions to Medical Psychology*, Vol. I, Pergamon Press, Oxford, 1977, and successive volumes.

2 Psychology and behavioral medicine

E. Blanchard, in R. Williams and W. Gentry (eds), *Behavioral Approaches to Medical Treatment*, Ballinger, Cambridge, 1977.

P. Ley, in S. Rachman (ed.), *Contributions to Medical Psychology*, Vol. I, Pergamon Press, Oxford, 1977.

3 Doctor's orders

B. Blackwell, British Journal of Psychiatry, 513 (1976).

4 Pain

R. Sternbach (ed.), *The Psychology of Pain*, Raven Press, New York, 1978, especially chap. 4, "Social Influences of Pain," by K. Craig.

M. Weisenberg (ed.), *The Control of Pain*, Psychological Dimensions, New York, 1977.

5 A psychological approach to headaches

D. Bakal, *Psychological Bulletin*, **83**, 367–83 (1975).

Clare Philips, A psychological analysis of tension headaches, in S. Rachman (ed.), *Contributions to Medical Psychology*, Vol. I, Pergamon Press, Oxford, 1977.

6 Sleep disorders

T. D. Borkovec, Insomnia, in R. B. Williams and W. D. Gentry (eds.), *Behavioral Approaches to Medical Treatment*, Ballinger, Cambridge, 1977.

7 *Placebo power*

A. Bergin and S. Garfield (eds.), *Handbook of Psychotherapy and Behavior Change,* 2nd ed., John Wiley, New York, 1978.

J. Herrick, *Psychological Reports,* **26,** 327 (1976).

8 *Self-control of bodily functions*

Biofeedback and Self-control, Aldine Annuals, Aldine, Chicago, successive issues.

E. B. Blanchard and W. Epstein, *A Primer of Biofeedback,* Addison-Wesley, Reading, Mass., 1978.

G. E. Schwartz and J. Beatty, *Biofeedback: Theory and Research,* Academic Press, New York, 1977.

9 *Reducing health risks by self-control*

D. Bernstein and A. MacAlister, *Addictive Behaviors,* **1,** 89 (1976).

P. Boudewyns, in R. Williams and W. Gentry (eds.), in *Behavioral Approaches to Medical Treatment,* Ballinger, Cambridge, 1977.

J. Foreyt (ed.), *Behavioral Treatments for Obesity,* Pergamon Press, Oxford, 1976.

M. Raw, in S. Rachman (ed.), *Contributions to Medical Psychology,* Vol. I, Pergamon Press, Oxford, 1977.

10 *Psychiatric psychology*

A. Clare, *Psychiatry in Dissent,* Tavistock Publications, London, 1977.

J. Maser and M. Seligman (eds.), *Psychopathology: Experimental Models,* W. H. Freeman, San Francisco, 1977.

S. Rachman and T. G. Wilson, *The Effects of Psychological Therapy,* 2nd ed., Pergamon Press, Oxford, 1980.

11 *The psychological impact of hospitalization*

B. Melamed, Psychological Preparation for Hospitalization, in S. Rachman (ed.), *Contributions to Medical Psychology,* Vol. I, Pergamon Press, Oxford, 1977.

12 *Health and stress*

B. Dohrenwend and B. Dohrenwend (eds.), *Stressful Life Events,* John Wiley, New York, 1974.

D. Glass and J. Singer, *Urban Stress,* Academic Press, New York, 1972.

J. Gray, *The Psychology of Fear and Stress*, Weidenfeld, London, 1971.
E. Gunderson and R. Rahe (eds.), *Life Stress and Illness*, Charles C Thomas, Springfield, Ill., 1974.
J. Rabkin and E. Streuning, *Science*, **194**, 1013 (1976).
H. Selye, *The Stress of Life*, McGraw-Hill, New York, 1978.

Index